MODELS OF FAMILY THERAPY: THE ESSENTIAL GUIDE

MODELS OF FAMILY THERAPY: THE ESSENTIAL GUIDE

William A. Griffin, Ph.D.
Shannon M. Greene, Ph.D.

Routledge
Taylor & Francis Group
LONDON AND NEW YORK

MODELS OF FAMILY THERAPY: The Essential Guide

First published 1999 by Routledge

Published 2016 by Routledge
2 Park Square, Milton Park, Abingdon, Oxon OX14 4RN
711 Third Avenue, New York, NY 10017, USA

Routledge is an imprint of the Taylor & Francis Group, an informa business

First issued in hardback 2015

Edited by Edward A. Cilurso and Jean Anderson. Printed by George H. Buchanan Co., Philadelphia, PA, 1998. Cover design by Joseph Dieter Visual Communications.

A CIP catalog record for this book is available from the British Library.

Library of Congress Cataloging-in-Publication Data

Available upon request from the publisher

ISBN 978-0-87630-886-8 (pbk)
ISBN 978-1-138-13532-1 (hbk)

CONTENTS

PREFACE

In this book we try to summarize each major family therapy model consistent with the way it was described originally. The summary is in outline form. While it is useful to read general overview texts of family therapy, there is no substitute for reading the inceptive work. By reviewing the original material and then presenting it in a semistructured outline form, we envision it functioning in three ways. First, this book can supplement other texts in a Marriage and Family Therapy course, or it can serve as the primary text supplemented by lecture. Second, graduate students can use it as a review guide for major exams. Finally, it can aid professionals who are preparing for any state or national examination on marriage and family therapy.

William A. Griffin
Shannon M. Greene

ACKNOWLEDGMENTS

This text would not have been possible without the support of National Institute of Mental Health grant 5 RO1 MH51184-03 and the fortunate opportunity to work with my friend, colleague, and coauthor, Shannon Greene. I also want to thank Sonia Krainz for her continuous support of me while I worked on this manuscript. She always knew when to push, and for that, I am indebted.

W.A.G.

I thank Bill Griffin for his generous invitation to collaborate on this book; it has been an enjoyable way to continue a long and valued friendship. I gratefully acknowledge support received from National Institute of Mental Health grant 2T32MH18387 for preparation of this manuscript. I am most appreciative of the love and support from my best friend and soul mate, Ed Anderson.

S.M.G.

The authors jointly thank Steve Rippon, Lisa Pain, and Laura Fichman for their editorial comments and helpful suggestions on earlier drafts of this text.

PART

I

AHISTORICAL MODELS

1

CHAPTER

Family Therapy Models: Structure and Rationale

This book provides an overview of established family therapy models. The guiding principle is *What are the critical components in each of the most prominent family therapy models?* In this text, critical component refers to information about a model that is essential to be conversant and literate. To obtain these components we distill each model down to a few core assumptions, terms, techniques, and methods.

Using a typology of family therapy models developed by Levant (1984) and modified by Griffin (1993), we put each model into one of three classifications: Ahistorical, Historical, or Experiential. Each classification represents a *general* orientation toward ameliorating the problem. Models within the Ahistorical classification attempt to remove the presenting problem by altering family interaction patterns. Advocates of this orientation assume that current interaction processes may be unrelated to the etiology of the presenting problem but certainly contribute to its maintenance. In general, the goal of therapy is to remove the presenting problem by changing attribution or behavioral patterns.

Historical models have a different set of characteristics. Each has psychoanalytic roots. Therapy tends to be longer and the therapist is generally less active in the session than in either of the other two classifications. Also important is individual growth and individuation within the family.

Experiential models are characterized by an emphasis on growth, experiencing and monitoring internal processes, and the development of self within the context of the family. In addition, therapists are encouraged to share their internal processes in response to the session. Additional information about the classifications is in Griffin (1993).

Any classification scheme of family therapy models must necessarily reduce ideological complexity, ignore overlap, and generalize for the purposes of category inclusion and exclusion. Nonetheless, orientation differences do exist, and it is usually helpful for the student or novice trainee to learn new material by placing ideas and methods into categories. To facilitate learning how the dimensions of each model "fit" with other models we have tried to enhance comparability by using the same general outline in all chapters. Each subsection within the outline is intended to answer the basic questions often asked by students and professionals new to family therapy. The outline format follows.

☐ Overview

Basic Summary

- This section of each chapter provides a one or two paragraph statement conveying the general model. Each Basic Summary section has four parts: Theory, Therapy, Therapist, and Training. Each section has several bullets explicating the assumptions in this topic area for this model.

Origin and Evolution

- We address how the model arose conceptually and historically. For some models, we also chronicle its intellectual genesis. For example, where pertinent, we attempt to briefly address (1) theoretical origins (e.g., single versus multiple influences and novel thought versus reaction to existing ideas); (2) geographical beginnings; (3) original contributors; and (4) theory evolution (e.g., changes in basic premises and application, current application form).

☐ Key Terms

- We define the terms typically associated with the model. Where relevant, we address how the term reflects or exemplifies the theoretical orientation.

☐ Key Techniques

- Here we describe the techniques needed within the model to implement client change. Where relevant, we discuss how the technique is an extension of the theory.

☐ Basic Tenets

How Do Problems Arise?

Here the question is, according to the model, what produces the presenting problem? Within the general answer, several additional questions are asked: What does the presenting problem reflect? What is the assumed connection between etiology and the presenting problem? What is the assumed functionality between the presenting problem and the system? If a function is assumed, how is it assessed (e.g., behavioral interactions, therapist sagacity)?

How Do Problems Persist?

Extending the prior section, this section addresses what the model posits as the conditions or behaviors that maintain the problem. Depending on the model, the techniques used in the model may be associated with the assumed etiological agent or the conditions assumed to be maintaining the problem.

What Is the Objective of Treatment?

This section addresses what the model assumes to be the goal of therapy. Depending on the model, this can range from clear behavioral change demanding removal of the presenting problem to an experiential change of oneself and its consequential alterations of interactions with others.

What Produces Change?

This section addresses what within the system must be altered in order for therapy to be successful. Somc models require a change in the microsocial interactions of family members, while others require that only one person change self-perception or attribution.

How Does Change Occur?

Here we identify the mechanism necessary to induce the change discussed in the prior section. That is, what must happen in- or out-of-session that alters the system sufficiently for therapy to be successful?

How Does Treatment Proceed?

Here we briefly outline the progression of therapy in this model. The outline provided in this section is very general and is only representative of the model with a nonspecific problem or family. Where possible, a step-by-step overview is given.

What Is the Role of the Therapist?

Each model differs in the prescribed role of the therapist. In this section, we provide an overview of the therapist's obligation to the change process within the model.

Several chapters include variants of the principal model. Some of the variants are more prominent or commonly used than their theoretical predecessor. These were included as variants rather than as separate models because their theoretical origins dictate that if you learn the principal model the variant follows naturally (e.g., Solution Focused follows from the Mental Research Institute model). That is, if you can think consistent with the premises of the original theory or model, the variant makes sense and is easy to remember.

To facilitate learning this material and to minimize confusion, we have avoided, or else defined, therapy jargon. We also rigorously sought to exclude polysyllabic psychobabble (e.g., neodeconstructivist ecosystemic epistemology). Sometimes a term or definition is unique to a model; when this occurs, we have tried to clearly define the word and illustrate its use in the model.

In addition, the text contains few references; instead, references for each chapter are in a special reference section in the back of the book. Symbols denote the relative importance of the reference. An E denotes essential readings and a B denotes beneficial readings. Essential readings delineate theoretical underpinnings; beneficial readings clarify and expand the model. We also have included a chapter of test questions to assist the reader in preparing for a Marriage and Family Therapy (MFT) test. These questions mirror those typically found at the graduate level and on standardized MFT tests.

Finally, the process of distilling the various models into their core components prohibited us from including therapy outcome research. As clinical research faculty we have an occupational bias toward research, yet a complete reporting of the assumptions and findings associated with family therapy outcome requires an extensive review of the literature. Because such a review exceeds the scope of this text, we instead list in the special reference section several recommended books and articles that should bring the reader up to date on the research literature. These are denoted with an F. In addition, we have provided a section, Additional Suggested Reading. Listed are several general texts and sourcebooks that should be in the library of any student in MFT. Each provides the reader a slightly different perspective of family therapy, and yet, collectively, they provide a good overview of the field. However, as noted in the Preface, *we recommend reading the originals*—then rely on general texts to provide a sense of the larger field.

2
CHAPTER

Structural Family Therapy

Overview

Structural Family Therapy assumes that functional families have compartmentalized yet accessible subunits arranged hierarchically with the parents on top. Behavior problems occur when either lack of adaptation to developmental changes or conflict within a subunit creates a faulty family structure. The therapist alters family interaction patterns during the session to correct the faulty family structure. After the presenting problem lessens or disappears, therapy stops. Structural Family Therapy is probably one of the most popular forms of family therapy because it has a clear theory, and the techniques are reasonable and easy to implement.

Basic Summary

Theory

- Behavior problems reflect inadequate family structure, usually resulting from a nonhierarchical arrangement of the parent and child subsystems.
- Inadequate family hierarchy occurs when the family members fail to recognize alternative patterns of engaging each other or when there is conflict between the parents.

Therapy

- The goal of therapy is to change boundaries and hierarchies sufficiently to remove or reduce the presenting problem.
- In-session tasks use humor, raise intensity, and reduce existing conflict by weakening existing patterns and installing new ones.

Therapist

- The therapist assesses where in the system the structure fails to carry out its function.
- The therapist then tries to disrupt the existing inadequate structure by forcing new interactions to occur during the session.
- The therapist alters the existing patterns by giving directives and demanding participation by the family members.

Training

- Personal therapy is not required.
- Live or videotaped supervision is common.
- Observation teams may be used.

Origin and Evolution

Salvador Minuchin, the founder of Structural Family Therapy, began his career in New York. His psychoanalytic training in psychiatry was at William Alanson White Institute, and his training in child psychiatry was at the Jewish Board of Guardians. He developed the principles of Structural Family Therapy during the early 1960s while at the Wiltwyck School for Boys. This facility dealt with young delinquents, mostly black and Puerto Rican. He left New York in early 1965 to be the director of the Philadelphia Child Guidance Clinic. He held this position for 10 years and then left in 1981.

During the 1960s, Minuchin's thinking shifted from a traditional psychodynamic view of human behavior to one reflecting a sociological perspective. This shift occurred contemporaneous to two ideas forwarded by Parsons and Bales (1955). First, the behavior of each family member influences and reflects family structure. Second, these behaviors also maintain the division of labor in the family; in turn, the division of labor maintains the structure. In short, the behavior of any family member serves to maintain structure. In effect, for example, a symptomatic child is expressing behavior that stabilizes the family.

The assumption that the presenting problem has a homeostatic function is still a cornerstone of the model. Consequently, structural family therapy occurs today as it did two decades ago.

Key Terms

Structure—behavior patterns organized to fulfill the functions of the family. Structural Family Therapy uses diagrams to illustrate family organization; these are shown in Figure 1.

Subsystems—one or more family members organized to carry out family roles. Subsystems are defined by redundant patterns organized across three dimensions:

- time,
- proximity,
- behavioral activity.

There are three primary subsystems:

- spousal,
- parental,
- child.

Boundaries—metaphorical barriers that surround subsystems. These barriers, categorized by their level of permeability, regulate the amount of contact with other subsystems. These categories are not discrete; instead, they describe a continuum of permeability and are described as follows:

Diffuse—the boundary is too permeable, resulting in minimum autonomy and individuation. Without autonomy, the subsystem does not carry out its needed functions. Individuals within these subsystems perceive a sense of emotional and psychological support but often fail to develop a sense of autonomy. A child, for example, does not engage in developmentally appropriate behaviors. Diffuse boundaries are associated with the concept *enmeshment*.

Clear—regulated and optimal amount of permeability.

Rigid—restrains contact with other subsystems. Rigid boundaries produce *disengaged* subsystems; these individuals are characterized by autonomy and independence but lack a sense of emotional and psychological support.

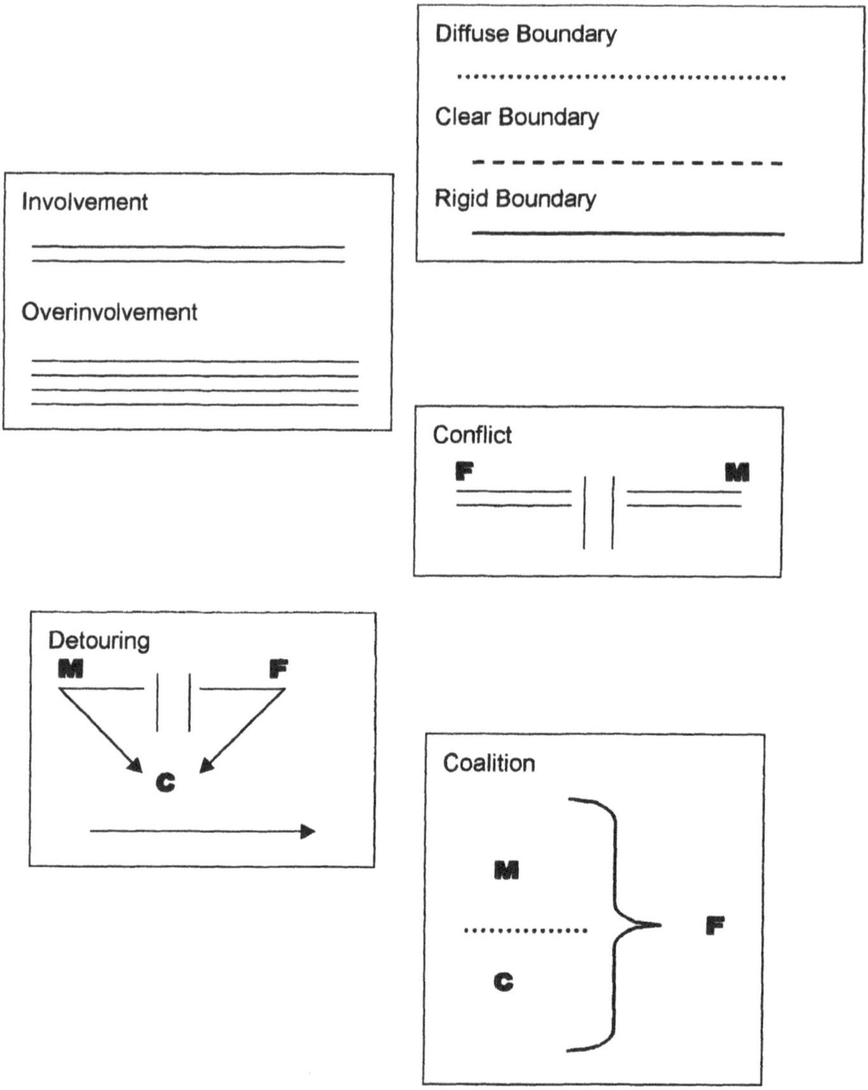

FIGURE 1. Symbols associated with Structural Family Therapy.

Hierarchy—the preferred ranking of subsystems; the parental subsystem should be above the child and sibling subsystems.

Power—the relative influence each family member has on the outcome of a system activity. Family members form coalitions to affect power.

Triangulation—the child's alliance with one parent against the other parent. This latter parent perceives the alliance as betrayal.

Coalition—two family members regularly join against a third. Triangulation always involves a child; a coalition may not. There are two types of coalitions:

- Inflexibility characterizes a *stable* coalition; the coalition does not vary across most family functions.
- Interpersonal conflict characterizes a *detouring* coalition; a third party is blamed for the discord. A detouring coalition functions to reduce stress in the stable coalition. Detouring coalitions have been suggested as a possible mechanism underlying psychosomatic illnesses (Minuchin, Rosman, & Baker, 1978).

Rules

- There are two types of rules: generic and idiosyncratic.
  - ➢ *Generic* (universal)—interaction patterns assumed to apply to all families. Families arrange themselves hierarchically, and parents show complementarity and reciprocity.
  - ➢ *Idiosyncratic* (individualized)—interaction patterns within a specific family. Patterns evolve over time, and, although not explicit, everyone knows they exist and can anticipate the consequences for a pattern violation.
- *Rule flexibility*—Flexibility in rules allows the system to accommodate normal transitions (e.g., birth of a child) and unexpected transitions (e.g., the death of a family member).

☐ Key Techniques

In-Session

Enactment—forcing the family to engage in behavioral patterns associated with the presenting problem. An enactment achieves the following outcome:

- raises in-session intensity
- destabilizes the system
- provides the therapist with
  - ➢ information about the family structure,
  - ➢ an opportunity to demonstrate that the current patterns are inadequate, and
  - ➢ an opportunity for a reframe.

Joining—therapist acts to increase family comfort by using the family's behaviors, language, and communication style. The therapist uses three primary techniques to join the family.

Accommodating—becoming part of the family system by using the family's thinking patterns, symbols, and organizational structure.

Tracking—using simple verbal and nonverbal behaviors that convey that the therapist is engaged and listening.

Mimesis—subtle mimicking of the family's affective and communication style.

Reframing (See Chapter 6, MRI, Key Techniques.)

Raising Intensity—The therapist manipulates affect intensity to destabilize patterned transactions within the family; only after the entrenched patterns are disrupted can new patterns be put in place consistent with the premises of this model. The Structural Family therapist has a mélange of in-session techniques to destabilize, unbalance, and raise intensity in the system; these include

- enactments (see definition above)
- adding or subtracting subsystems
- forming new cross-generational coalitions
- altering the symptom—
  - ➢ exaggerating the symptom
  - ➢ deemphasizing the symptom
  - ➢ moving to a new symptom
  - ➢ relabeling the symptom
- reinforcing spontaneous behavior sequences
- using temporal or physical distance to reinforce boundaries (e.g., moving chairs or family members)
- using goal-specific tasks that force new transactions

Out-of-Session

Although rare, some out-of-session tasks occur. Their implementation concretizes the new behavior patterns instigated in-session.

Basic Tenets

How Do Problems Arise?

Dysfunctional behavior arises from inadequate family structure. At least two mechanisms produce this inadequacy:

- lack of appropriate reconfiguration concomitant with
  - ➢ life stage developmental changes;
  - ➢ unexpected major changes in family composition (e.g., death of a child);
  - ➢ major environmental changes (e.g., job move, teacher conflicts); and
- evolving conflict in the parental relationship.

Each scenario above requires structural accommodation to the situation. With incompetent accommodation, actions taken in response to the inadequate structure are functionally appropriate but behaviorally inappropriate. When this occurs, a symptom emerges. Structural therapy assumes that the symptom

- signals a structural deficit (e.g., inability to adjust to development changes),
- deflects intrasubsystem conflict onto a scapegoat thereby stabilizing an unstable situation by focusing attention away from the subsystem, and
- retards normal developmental maturation.

How Do Problems Persist?

Although an identified patient (IP) is designated, the problem does not reside within the individual. Rather the individual manifests behavior reflecting inadequate family structure. The IP in this model represents the system—aberrant behavior reflects inadequate structure. The continued expression of problem behavior, or even psychosomatic illness, represents the fulfillment of actions consistent with the faulty structure.

What Is the Objective of Therapy?

Removing the symptom is the goal of therapy. This occurs when thc faulty family structure changes sufficiently to stop dysfunctional transactions.

What Produces Change?

Change occurs by introducing transactional patterns that reinforce appropriate hierarchies and strengthen boundaries. These structural changes alter the assumed or assessed structural deficit.

How Does Change Occur?

Change occurs when the therapist uses in-session techniques to alter the way family members interact. Theory assumes that in-session transaction pattern deviations will force structural reorganization and that these changes will generalize to the home environment. The therapist also challenges and attempts to modify attributional sets and beliefs that inhibit the needed structural changes.

How Does Treatment Proceed?

Initial Sessions

- Join the family:
  - accommodation,
  - tracking,
  - mimesis.
- Assess family structure:
  - asking questions;
  - using enactments;
  - watching interactions for
    - cross-generational coalitions,
    - interparental conflict,
    - inadequate boundaries between subsystems.
- Attend to the presenting problem.
- Assume that the family has available but unused alternative methods of interacting.
- Raise intensity strategically.
- Give directives that restructure the family system by
  - reinforcing good transactions;
  - expanding the repertoire of transactional patterns available to the family;
  - challenging behavioral patterns, not individuals;
  - challenging the family's perception of the problem;
  - using reframes.

Subsequent Sessions

- Create objectives:
  - ➢ Small changes in interactions are accepted as progress.
  - ➢ Therapy attempts to develop
    - ♦ an effective hierarchy with an executive coalition,
    - ♦ clear boundaries.
  - ➢ Devise system level structures that
    - ♦ are appropriate for the family's developmental stage,
    - ♦ allow age-appropriate individuation.
- Termination of treatment is appropriate when
  - ➢ the presenting problem is gone,
  - ➢ the structure supporting the symptom has changed, and
  - ➢ structural flexibility allows future adaptation to changes.

What Is the Role of the Therapist?

The therapist is responsible for forcing the family to change their interaction patterns. To induce this change, the therapist

- is active;
- gives directives;
- is quick to give positive reinforcement;
- uses humor;
- infrequently uses self, giving advice only if strategically useful.

Family structure is manipulated at two levels, the overt and the covert. The therapist

- overtly manipulates the family structure by
  - ➢ raising intensity,
  - ➢ use of enactments,
  - ➢ moving people and furniture,
  - ➢ commenting on and altering process;
- covertly manipulates the family structure by
  - ➢ posing questions that focus on structure and the desired structural change,
  - ➢ challenging attributional sets.

3

CHAPTER

Strategic Family Therapy

☐ Overview

Strategic therapy refers to a group of therapies characterized by an active, directive therapist who attempts, through prescribed tasks, to alter interaction patterns around the presenting problem (Haley, 1973). This is strategic therapy in the general sense (i.e., lowercase "s" strategic) and includes Solution Focused Therapy (de Shazer, 1985), Narrative approaches (White & Epston, 1990), Communication approaches (see Chapter 6, MRI; Watzlawick, 1990), and Jay Haley's Strategic Family Therapy. In the specific case (i.e., capital "S" strategic), Strategic Family Therapy primarily refers to the specific body of work created by Jay Haley (1963, 1973, 1980, 1984, 1987). Although primarily associated with Haley, this model also includes the writings of Madanes (1981, 1984, 1990), Hoffman (1981), and Stanton (1981).

Haley's Strategic Family Therapy integrates Ericksonian hypnotherapeutic techniques (Haley, 1973, 1981), Mental Research Institute's (MRI's) emphasis on systems and cybernetics (Watzlawick, 1990), and Minuchin's ideas of subsystem boundaries and family hierarchy (Minuchin, 1974). In practice, therapy consists of problem identification, assessment of the behavioral sequences surrounding the problem, and then the assignment of tasks to alter systematically the associated sequences. Subsequent sessions address compliance, offering new tasks that attempt to continue altering the identified problem sequences.

Basic Summary

Theory

- A symptom occurs when there is a power struggle in the system, because of either an inadequate hierarchy or conflict between two individuals.
- Symptoms reflect specific behavioral interactions in the family. Small incremental shifts in behavioral sequence can
  - reestablish appropriate hierarchies,
  - reduce conflict, and
  - abate power struggles.
- Individuals or families have the psychological resources to self-correct if provided the opportunity via therapy.
- A symptom is a metaphor for the larger organization.

Therapy

- The goal of therapy is to remove the presenting problem.
- Therapy tries to make small systematic changes in the social interactions that are associated with the defined problem.

Therapist

- The therapist develops strategies that will change the family's interaction sufficient to remove the presenting problem.
- The therapist is responsible for implementing change in the family.

Training

- Personal therapy is not required.
- Live or videotaped supervision is common.

Origin and Evolution

Beginning in the mid-1950s, Haley was in a unique position to cultivate, articulate, and eventually integrate three distinct psychotherapy orientations (Grove & Haley, 1993). Initially, Haley was the primary biographer of Erickson (Haley, 1973), articulating positions on therapist control and responsibility and the need to create specific behavioral tasks. Next, as an early member of the MRI staff, Haley helped develop many of the techniques that became associated with the Communication/MRI model. Finally, in

1967 Haley moved to Philadelphia to work with Minuchin at the Philadelphia Child Guidance Clinic. During the seven years in Philadelphia, Haley incorporated some new ideas about family structure and hierarchy into his existing Ericksonian and MRI style. After moving to Rockville, Maryland, Haley and Cloe Madanes started the Family Therapy Institute in 1974.

While Haley has changed little since his early writings, Madanes has moved away from traditional strategic techniques into the realm of humanistic strategic. In the early 1980s, Madanes (1981, 1984) wrote that children alter family interactions through symptoms because they are unable to directly help their parents' marriage. Treatment focused on helping the children directly communicate with the parent(s), which made the symptoms unnecessary. More recently, Madanes (1990, 1991) wrote that symptoms reflect issues of love and violence in the family. This shift makes the work of Madanes substantially different from traditional Strategic.

☐ Key Terms

There are only a few unique terms associated with Strategic, and most are associated with specific techniques (see Key Techniques). However, the following common family therapy terms have unique meaning in this model.

Power—in Strategic terms, "He who makes the rules has the power." Addresses who in the system is in the position to make decisions about rules. At its root, power is a concept associated with organizational hierarchy.

Triangle—assumes that problems occur when a power struggle between two people forces the involvement of a third person. The third person may be evident, as in a symptom-bearing child, or may go unidentified or acknowledged. This assumption requires the therapist to conceptualize all marital therapy interventions in terms of at least three people (Haley, 1987).

☐ Key Techniques

Although Strategic is known for indirect, paradoxical, and ordeal techniques, most of the strategies are direct, straightforward, and tractable. Below is a list of some of the techniques associated with Strategic Family Therapy.

Ordeals—The therapist attaches an aversive, yet constructive, activity to the presenting problem. If the presenting problem occurs, the client must do the activity. If, for example, an adolescent boy has a habit of coming home after curfew, he might be required to walk the dogs around the neighborhood—all four dogs, one at a time.

Paradoxical (Haley, 1987)

- prescribing the symptom—therapist instructs the client to engage in problem behavior;
- restraining the change—therapist tries to deny the possibility of change, or argues that the pace of change should be slowed;
- positioning—therapist tries to shift the client's conceptualization of the problem by exaggerating it.

Reframing (See Chapter 6, MRI, Key Techniques.)

Positive Connotations (See Chapter 6, Milan, Key Terms.)

Manipulating the Symptom (See Chapter 6, MRI, Key Techniques.)

☐ Basic Tenets

General Assumptions

Family Structure

- Functional families have clear organizational hierarchy with the parents in charge.
- A bad marriage is usually, but not always, associated with the presenting problem. It is not advisable or necessary to address the marriage in therapy; simply altering relevant behavioral sequences is sufficient to stop the problem.
- Because the inadequate structure conveys itself through the problem, the symptom is a metaphor for the system.
- The triangle is the basic building block of any emotional interpersonal system.

Change

- Individuals and families have psychological resources that will enable them to change.
- Resistance to change is a natural by-product of stability; in therapy it should be expected and used to facilitate change.
- Rigid sequences of behaviors restrict the family's ability to change; not all elements in the identified sequence need altering; only enough altering is needed to instigate change.
- Developing insight in patients is unimportant to solving problems.
- Problems in the identified patient cannot be expected to change unless the family system changes.
- People can change quickly, and therapy can be brief.

Power and Control

- Control is not defined as the manipulation of another individual, but instead it refers to the ability to determine the definition of the relationship. In other words, conflict reflects the struggle to define the nature (i.e., rules) of a relationship within a family (see Power; Key Terms). Whoever controls the definition of the relationship controls the relationship (e.g., "What will our relationship consist of?").
- Helplessness, incompetence, and illness provide a position of power in the family (Madanes, 1981).

How Do Problems Arise?

The presenting problem is the result of a behavioral sequence occurring in the social organization of the immediate group. This sequence evolves because of a power struggle in the system. These struggles are due to either an inadequate hierarchy or conflict between two individuals. The symptom may also reflect the latter stage of earlier attempts to fix the problem that were not successful using more conventional means (Haley, 1963). Families are most vulnerable to these struggles during normal life transitions when family rules are either rigid or inadequate. In addition, behavior problems may extend beyond a family problem; for example, they may be interwoven into more abstract issues of parental, social, and economic hardships.

How Do Problems Persist?

Rigid behavioral sequences maintain the problem. Once these sequences become established, the symptoms associated with the problem act as homeostatic mechanisms regulating family interaction patterns.

What Is the Objective of Therapy?

Removing the presenting problem is the goal of therapy. This removal occurs by changing the behavioral sequences associated with the presenting problem. Moreover, altering the relevant behavioral patterns changes the current hierarchical structure. In short, since behavioral sequences maintain the problem, if you alter the sequence, you change the problem.

What Produces Change?

Change occurs when the family engages in a new behavioral sequence that is incompatible with the one associated with the presenting problem. This shift in sequence occurs in small increments; each incremental modification reflects the amount of behavior change mandated by the assigned task.

How Does Change Occur?

Change occurs when the therapist assigns out-of-session tasks to the family. These tasks require small but systematic changes in the identified behavioral sequence associated with the presenting problem. Sometimes the Strategic therapist will reframe the symptom in order to increase compliance. Assigned tasks usually have an unambiguous relationship with the symptom: the family sees a clear connection between the requested change and the presenting problem.

How Does Treatment Proceed?

Haley (1987) divides the initial interview into five stages:

Social Stage—greet and make family members comfortable;

Problem Stage—inquire about the presenting problem;

Interaction Stage—ask family members to talk with each other;

Goal-Setting Stage—ask each family member to specify what he or she wants changed, and;

Task-Setting Stage—give a directive. The initial interview ends after the next appointment is set. Depending on therapist preferences, the directive given, and the presenting problem, the entire family or only a few members schedule for the next session.

Below is a brief description of each stage.

The Social Stage

The therapist has several objectives at this stage.

- Get as many relevant people as possible into therapy.
- Find out
  - ➢ names,
  - ➢ ages,
  - ➢ occupations,
  - ➢ addresses,
  - ➢ telephone numbers of the relevant persons,
  - ➢ who lives in the household,
  - ➢ who has had previous therapy,
  - ➢ who referred the family.
- Observe and assess
  - ➢ mood of the family;
  - ➢ how the parent(s) deals with the children as they enter the room and begin the session;
  - ➢ how family members organize themselves
    - ♦ physically in the room,
    - ♦ conceptually around the presenting problem (i.e., who sides with or against whom);
  - ➢ how family members perceive the therapist;
  - ➢ the behavior of other family members while each individual talks.
- Establish rapport.
- If a child problem presents, assume that adults in the family, in some measure, disagree about how to handle the problem.
- Keep conclusions tentative, and refuse to share conclusions and recommendations too soon.
- Avoid diagnostic labels.

The Problem Stage

At this stage, the therapist needs to let a problem definition develop. This occurs via questions.

The Problem

- What is the problem (asked of all family members)?
- What do you want changed (family level question)?
- What do you expect from the therapist (family level question)?

Listening to the Problem

- Avoid
  - ➢ commenting on the client's perspective of the problem—listen;
  - ➢ offering advice at this point—stall until the latter stages;
  - ➢ asking about feelings—stick to facts and opinions;
  - ➢ being detached—show helpful interest.
- Focus on
  - ➢ the present; history is relevant only to the presenting problem;
  - ➢ process (interaction sequences) rather than content (what is said);
  - ➢ who is *most* invested in change;
  - ➢ who is *least* invested in change.

The Interaction Stage

There are two steps to asking about the problem.

- Force all family members to comment on the problem.
- Force the interactions associated with the problem to occur in the room (similar to Structural Family Therapy's enactment).

Goal-Setting Stage

- Define clear specific goals—a therapeutic contract is being constructed between the therapist and client.
- Get and maintain compliance by focusing on the presenting problem.
- Focus changes on the person associated with the problem while simultaneously altering behaviors of multiple individuals associated with the problem.
- Quantify all behaviors associated with the goals—they must be measurable to all parties.

Task-Setting Stage

- Assign tasks that make small systematic changes in the social interactions associated with the defined problem. Each individual directly involved in the therapy needs to have a subjective experience of the problem after having done the task.

Subsequent Sessions

- Assess compliance with the previous task and give a new task.

- Make an intervention and see how the family responds is a system level diagnosis.
  - ➢ Task compliance and noncompliance provide information about the system.
  - ➢ Any outcome is information used in subsequent task assignment.

Haley's General Formula for Successful Therapy

- Know what you want and be precise.
- Assign everyone something to do relative to changing the interactions.
- Start with small changes using at-home tasks.
- Know the family well enough to anticipate what may go wrong.
- Develop a task that gets compliance from the family.

What Is the Role of the Therapist?

From the onset of therapy, the therapist is responsible for implementing change. Lack of change reflects the therapist's inability to comprehend the situation and client sufficiently to implement a good strategy that shifts behavior (Griffin, 1993). The therapist motivates and challenges the client. He or she directs in-session behavior and dictates, via tasks, what should occur out-of-session. Without being abrupt or short, the therapist is responsible for the direction of therapy and is, therefore, insistent that in-session behavior be directed toward solving the presenting problem. The therapist does not tell people what they are doing wrong; instead the therapist has them engage in behavior that provides a new perspective of the problem. When change does not occur, the therapist accepts the postulate that he or she has not found the right wording or task sufficient to induce change.

Haley has written extensively about expected therapist behavior. Below is a summary of his ideas.

- The therapist
  - ➢ uses family value structure and culture to devise effective tasks;
  - ➢ is creative in devising tasks and directives;
  - ➢ modifies the presenting problem through intermediate goals; small changes lead to larger changes;
  - ➢ alters the perception of the presenting problem in order to make it amenable to modification;
  - ➢ uses any technique as long as it might work to change behavioral sequences;
  - ➢ is responsible for defining the social or familial unit so that it involves enough people for change in relevant behavior sequences;

- ➢ integrates into the system's definition of the problem merely by
  - ♦ asking about the problem under the guise of being able to help,
  - ♦ attending to client responses,
  - ♦ suggesting how the problem can be fixed;
- ➢ is cognizant of how his or her role in the problem alters the proposed remedy;
- ➢ assumes
  - ♦ that asking a family how they feel does not change experience, but changing experience will change how they feel,
  - ♦ that clients who have been in therapy before will often try to direct therapy, and if allowed, the therapy is as unsuccessful as the previous therapy experience,
  - ♦ that delivery is at least as important as the task itself,
  - ♦ that he or she has the ability to make a bad situation worse by
    - ▪ ignoring information,
    - ▪ presenting the problem to the family incompetently; this can potentially concretize a problem and increase the odds of chronicity.

Cloe Madanes

Although their initial work was very similar, Madanes has moved away from the thinking typically associated with Haley. Several of her unique assumptions place her in a variant category of traditional Strategic Family Therapy.

The first is her emphasis of helplessness as power. Madanes sees helplessness as an opportunity to manipulate social behavior. Madanes considers this a particularly powerful position because it is nonarguable; being sick or anxiety stricken is not something that others can take lightly. Another shift is her emphasis on the client's pretending to either have or not have the symptom. Compliance in either direction implies control over the symptom. With a sense of control comes an alternative perspective of the problem, a desired shift by the strategic therapist.

Finally, Madanes assumes that all problems presented to therapy result from the dilemma between love and violence (Madanes, 1990). Family problems, according to her, result from one of four struggles: each struggle expresses itself in a particular type of problem—

- behavioral problems result from a desire to dominate and control others;
- psychosomatic, affective, and anxiety disorders stem from the desire to be loved;
- violence, abuse, neglect, and suicide stem from the desire to be loved; and
- incest comes from the desire to repent and forgive.

With these assumptions as the basis for treatment, Madanes attempts to alter behavioral sequences so that family members can interact without resorting to manipulation (e.g., faking an illness) to get attention and love. This shift moves the work of Madanes from brief, goal-oriented therapy to a form of (typically brief) humanistic-strategic therapy.

4

CHAPTER

Behavioral Family Therapy

Overview

This model assumes that an individual's behavior reflects a complex, cumulative process of learning. Because children learn from their parents, parenting skills are the assumed culprit if the presenting problem is a child's behavior. Also relevant to the presenting problem is anything that reinforces, extinguishes, or predisposes an individual to exhibit a behavior (Bandura, 1978). This includes not only intrafamilial agents (e.g., parenting skills, family belief systems, marital quality, adult dysfunction), but other possible factors such as stress, genetic predisposition, and social context (e.g., neighborhoods) as well. Treatment consists of teaching monitoring skills, adding and improving behavior management skills, and increasing positive reinforcement of good behaviors along with the extinction of undesired behaviors.

Basic Summary

Theory

- Behavior is learned, both deviant and prosocial.
- Aggressive and coercive behavior
  - ➢ begins in the family, and
  - ➢ is eventually maintained by peers.

- Effective parenting skills can be taught; these skills
  - will be implemented by most motivated parents, and
  - will reduce offensive behaviors if implemented effectively.

Therapy

- The goal of therapy is to remove the presenting problem.
- All interventions have four components:
  - data collection via observation;
  - construction of hypothesized relationships among relevant variables;
  - an intervention based on the hypotheses; and
  - evaluation of the intervention.
- Parents are taught
  - monitoring,
  - appropriate behavior reinforcement and extinction skills,
  - responsibility for controlling the child's environment.
- Specific behaviors are targeted for change.
- Limited number of sessions.

Therapist

- A teacher of skills and consultant to the parents.
- Takes responsibility for getting the parents to implement the new skills.

Training

- Personal therapy is not required.
- Skilled at behavior reinforcement and methodology.

Origin and Evolution

The most visible beginning of Behavioral Family Therapy was the 1971 publication of Gerald Patterson's *Families*. In this book, he outlines very specific procedures for increasing parenting skills:

- learning to observe,
- pinpointing specific behaviors,
- establishing a baseline,
- graphing the behavior,
- negotiating a contract, and
- using time-out properly.

Although the requisite parenting skills have not changed since the 1970s, an additional component has been added—acceptance of cognitions as mediating agents between overt behavior and the associated attributional set among family members. This acceptance has at least two implications. First, the parental report and interpretation of child behavior is reactive, subject to emotion and situational influences. Thus, parent report is fallible. Second, family members respond in part to the behavior and, in part, to its meaning as determined by its use within the family.

This shift forced Behavioral Family Therapy to examine the behavior's meaning among the individuals involved in the problem behavior. Consequently, appreciating the behavior's meaning has become an integral part of the treatment plan.

☐ Key Terms

Assessment—Behavioral Family Therapy assesses the problem and the family in a systematic and scientific manner. Several key features of assessment are associated with the model; it

- focuses on overt behavior,
- accounts for attributional processes and environmental factors that influence the attributions (e.g., job stress, perceived economic conditions),
- requires an examination of antecedents, behaviors (problem), and consequences (ABCs),
- requires a detailed analysis of the behaviors that need increasing and decreasing,
- monitors variations in the presenting problem along with the behaviors that are thought to influence the problem,
- occurs at in-take and during treatment,
- determines treatment effectiveness, not client or therapist report.

Coercive Interactions—the process of parent request ⇒ aversive child response ⇒ parent acquiesce; child is reinforced for noncompliance, concretizing a coercive negativity-based parent–child interaction style.

Reciprocity—the equitable exchange of positives or negatives among family members. It is assumed, for example, that family members will, on average, return (reciprocate) behaviors of the same valence and at the same rate; that is, a negative will prompt a negative response.

Behavior Modification

- Extinction—lack of reward reduces an undesired. behavior
- Operant conditioning—uses reinforcers to alter the subsequent likelihood of a behavior. There are two forms of reinforcement:

- ➢ *Positive:* increase the frequency of a behavior by pairing something of value with the completion of the desired behavior; reward is contingent on behavior (or close approximate) being done.
- ➢ *Negative:* increase in behavior obtained by the removal of an aversive stimuli; seldom used in Behavioral Family Therapy.

☐ Key Techniques

General Parenting Skills Training

- Education—developmental information.
- Charting—graphing monitored behavior and rewards.
- Time-out—extinguishing behavior by isolating the child from stimuli and reinforcers.
- Modeling—demonstrating appropriate behavior; therapist for parent, parent for child.
- Shaping—Parents reinforce desired behaviors through successive approximations.
- Role playing and behavioral rehearsal—practicing desirable behavioral scenarios in-session.
- Communication skills training—paraphrasing, "I" statements, etc. Problem solving skills training—brainstorming, goal setting, etc.

Contingency Contracting—a contract outlining desired and undesired behaviors, characterized by

- explicitly stated expectations, rewards, and punishments;
- negotiation among parties;
- some portion addresses decreasing negative behavior;
- emphasis on
  - ➢ mutual responsibility,
  - ➢ increase in positives.

☐ Basic Tenets

How Do Problems Arise?

Two theories underpin Behavioral Family Therapy—social learning and social exchange. Social learning provides a structure for the process of acquiring behavior (Bandura, 1978, 1982), and social exchange theory provides a framework for understanding behavioral actions over the long term (Thibaut & Kelly, 1959). Together, these theories provide the framework for applying behavioral principles to behavior problems in children, especially antisocial boys. Using these theories to frame empirical data, Gerald Patterson, John Reid, Tom Dishion, and colleagues postulate the following stages in the development of antisocial boys (see Patterson, Reid, & Dishion, 1992):

- Family members, especially parents, are the trainers for inappropriate aggressive and antisocial behavior. It begins in the home, and it occurs before adolescence. The process begins with confrontations between parent and child during discipline. Over time these conflict bouts increase in duration and intensity and eventually expand to include siblings.
- When these children reach school age, peers reject many of them because of the behaviors brought from home. If the child does not adapt to the school environment either academically or socially, he or she is at much higher risk for behavior problems.
- At-risk children tend to find each other in school. Without close parental monitoring, they spend increasing time together, polishing and refining their antisocial skills.

While some proportion of these children will adjust and move toward the mainstream of accepted behavior, a substantial proportion will have a difficult and marginal existence in adulthood. Data clearly show higher lifetime risk for unemployment, drug and alcohol problems, arrests, and marital difficulties.

How Do Problems Persist?

Once established, inadequate skills and inappropriate reinforcement maintain most problems. For example, data show that the following behaviors characterize families with problem children (see Patterson et al., 1992):

- High levels of
  - ➢ noncontingent reinforcement (i.e., parent reinforces the child irrespective of the appropriateness of the child's behavior),
  - ➢ inept discipline,
  - ➢ negative tracking (i.e., parents only notice the bad behavior),
  - ➢ aversive interactions,
  - ➢ coercive processes.
- Low levels of
  - ➢ positive tracking (i.e., parents watch for and reward good behavior),
  - ➢ clearly defined rules about behavior and responsibility,
  - ➢ appropriate praise,
  - ➢ monitoring,

- ➢ parent involvement,
- ➢ positive reinforcement.

This model also assumes that some children have a constitutional predisposition (i.e., temperament) for antisocial or aggressive behavior and that the behavior can be modified by appropriate parental skills (Falloon, 1991). Conversely, inappropriate or inadequate parenting may exacerbate a predisposition—a temperamentally difficult child with a stern, inflexible parent is a blueprint for behavioral difficulties.

What Is the Objective of Therapy?

Therapy attempts to remove or alter impediments to effective parenting sufficient to alleviate the presenting problem. The client, not the therapist, determines the goal of therapy. Rather than specify what the client should have as a goal, the model specifies only how the therapist implements change. In short, the objective of therapy is to alter current behavior patterns and to reduce or modify symptoms sufficient to please the client.

What Produces Change?

Change occurs when the parents alter environment contingencies that control the behavior. A singular objective is to determine environmental control of the behavior, and Behavioral Family Therapy assumes that parents exert much control over the environment.

How Does Change Occur?

Change occurs when the therapist alters the environmental contingencies tied to the problem. The problem reduces to three behavioral features: antecedents, behaviors (problem), and consequences (ABCs). After assessment, change occurs by

- reducing or varying antecedents associated with the problem;
- teaching alternative ways of responding to the problem; and
- altering the consequences.

This latter component is necessary especially to reduce the negative escalation cycle in couples and families (see Crane (1996) for a discussion of marital therapy). Manipulation of these three components requires skill acquisition (at least from the behavioral perspective because it assumes that, if present, the skills would evidence themselves). Recent evidence clearly indicates that this is not true—skill use diminishes during periods of stress (Wahler & Dumas, 1989). In addition, this model assumes that a reduction of negative affect expression does not imply that positive affect will increase.

How Does Treatment Proceed?

Initial Session(s)

- A problem behavior is targeted and defined.
- Targeted behavior is assessed:
  - ➢ obtain history,
  - ➢ determine who is associated with the problem.
- The contingencies of the targeted behavior are determined:
  - ➢ antecedents;
  - ➢ consequences;
  - ➢ response characteristics
    - ♦ duration,
    - ♦ frequency,
    - ♦ location.
- Involves a behavioral interview and behavioral checklists that may involve analog (e.g., lab) and naturalistic (e.g., home) observations.
- Assumes that covariations exist between subsystems; movement or change in one subunit affects other subunits.
- Goals are established for the targeted behavior. They must be
  - ➢ clearly defined, consisting of behaviors that are observable and countable;
  - ➢ realistic;
  - ➢ age appropriate; and
  - ➢ consistent with family traditions.
- Parents are taught specific parenting skills based on their assumed deficit; these would always include
  - ➢ monitoring;
  - ➢ positive tracking and reinforcement:
    - ♦ problem solving,
    - ♦ effective discipline tactics (e.g., time-out, contracting); and
    - ♦ increased parent involvement.

Subsequent Sessions

After initial sessions, the objective is to monitor and evaluate skill change and modify contracts and reinforcers as necessary. Assessment occurs throughout the treatment period to determine if and how relevant parent–child interactions change because of treatment. Behavioral Family Therapy typically contracts for a limited number of sessions, negotiating for more sessions as new problems emerge.

Behavioral Family Therapy does not immediately assume that the marriage is distressed if a child misbehaves. Instead, it assumes that the parents are not parenting well and will proceed with parent training. Only after failure, usually because of parent noncompliance, does the therapist probe for possible marital difficulties. Dysfunctional patterns of interaction represent the best efforts to respond to the current circumstances, given the skill level and motivation among family members. This assumes that

- parents have the capacity to generate change;
- the primary reason for treatment failure in Behavioral Family Therapy is parental inconsistency;
- parents can, and will, fail to implement treatment;
- marital dissatisfaction and adult psychopathology adversely influence treatment outcome; and
- both parents should exhibit a consistent reinforcement pattern that appears unified to the child.

What Is the Role of the Therapist?

The therapist is responsible for getting the parents to change their parenting behaviors. Treatment fails when the therapist does not provide the relevant behavior change techniques to the family. It also occurs when the therapist asks for change too quickly or is inattentive to the client's verbal and nonverbal hesitancy of change (Patterson & Chamberlain, 1988). Within this model, the therapist is

- not involved directly with the child; instead the expectation is established that parents will implement behavior change techniques;
- an educator or technical consultant to the parents.

☐ Variants

Functional Family Therapy

In the mid 1970s, Jim Alexander and colleagues at the University of Utah were the first to combine Behavioral Family Therapy with a general systems approach (Alexander & Parsons, 1982; Barton & Alexander, 1981). Calling the approach Functional Family Therapy, it was premised on the idea that family interactions function to regulate degrees of merging (desire for closeness) and separating (independence). The therapy process involves determining how the behavior of an individual (or a family) is functional in controlling intimacy. A therapist in this model examines and clarifies problem behaviors, reframes and relabels the behavior so that each family member can understand how the behavior functions within the family, and illustrates with discussions and homework assignments how such behaviors are interdependent among family members.

Cognitive Behavioral Therapy with Couples and Families

As noted in the beginning of this chapter, behaviorists working with families have shifted from a pure stimulus–response mentality to one that incorporates cognitions as mediators of behavior. Likewise, behavioral therapists working with couples have incorporated cognitions as essential components to any behavior change treatment program (Baucom & Epstein, 1990). Work in this area has identified at least two major nonexclusive domains relevant to the cognitive therapist: (1) cognitions and beliefs brought into the marriage from the family of origin (Dattilio & Padesky, 1990; Dattilio, 1998); and (2) current faulty beliefs, held by each spouse, that contribute to marital discord (Epstein, Baucom, & Daiuto, 1997).

From the family of origin, each individual brings to the relationship a cognitive schema. This schema reflects assumptions, attributions, and cognitions constructed from perceptions of relationship dynamics in the family of origin and, in general, in all previous relationships. This cognitive map establishes the baseline for evaluating all interspousal interactions. Logically, if two individuals bring disparate schemas into the marriage the likelihood of discord is high. Moreover, a modified schema evolves as the relationship evolves. This new schema is influenced by contemporaneous cognitions, some concordant with the existing relationship, others discordant. These discordant cognitions are the primary focus of the cognitive behavioral therapist. According to Epstein et al. (1997), five types of cognitions are applicable to intimate relationships:

- assumptions: about relationships (defined about);
- standards: how relationships and partners "should" be;
- selective attention: systematic bias in attending behavior;
- attributions: inferences about cause in the partner's behavior;
- expectancies: inferences about future behavior in the partner.

If any of the five types of cognitions is faulty, the relationship suffers. The therapist using logic and questions exposes faulty thinking patterns. Combining cognitive change strategies with the usual behavioral changes techniques, the therapist attempts to alter simultaneously the thinking and the behaving of the couple.

Sex Therapy

Before the work of Masters and Johnson (1970) there was limited treatment for sexual dysfunction. With the publication of their seminal work, Masters and Johnson effectively began the field of sex therapy. Other prominent writers in this field include Kaplan (1974) and LoPiccolo & LoPiccolo

(1978). Although sexual dysfunction is a problem for an individual, in the realm of treatment, it is a dyadic problem. This shift from viewing and treating sexual dysfunction as possessed by an individual to a characteristic of a couple clearly moves dysfunction from person to system. Also, irrespective of theoretical orientation (e.g., Kaplan is psychodynamic), treatment follows a very behavioral or cognitive–behavioral paradigm. Most investigators in this area view sexual dysfunction, aside from organic problems, to be a product of anxiety. The anxiety either preceded the dysfunction or is concurrent with it; irrespective of when it appeared, anxiety and the fear of failing stifles an otherwise natural process.

Although treatment may vary by practitioner, the general format is consistent across clinics:

- initial interview to get a definition and description of the problem, followed by a through medical examination;
- this is followed by an extensive sexual history with both parties;
- depending on the presenting problem and the sexual knowledge of the couple, the next stage might include information about physiological processes associated with sex and how they are influenced by anxiety;
- most treatments begin by teaching the couple to employ sexual pleasuring without the pressure to actually engage in intercourse or have an orgasm; this technique is called *sensate focus.* Sensate focus is actually a series of gradated couple exercises that starts with simple touching accompanied by a discussion of the resulting feelings and sensations. Subsequent exercises progress to increasing levels of intimacy. At each level, the couple examines feelings and thoughts that occur with the behaviors. The general purpose of these exercises is to reduce sexual anxiety, but there is an additional benefit to couples—it allows them to interact differently in what previously had been a dissatisfying domain of the relationship.
- After the sensate focus exercises are complete, the therapist usually assigns a specific sexual technique or exercise for the presenting problem. For example, for premature ejaculation, the couple is taught the squeeze technique or Kaplan's (1987) Stop–Start technique. A large number of specific remedies have been developed for most sexual dysfunctions (see, e.g., Kaplan, 1987).

5

CHAPTER

Psychoeducational Family Therapy

Overview

Psychoeducational Family Therapy was originally designed for use with schizophrenics released from inpatient facilities (Anderson, 1983). With the goal of improving patient functioning by reducing family stress, this model typically covers education about the illness, family-level psychotherapeutic interventions (e.g., skills training or structural/behavioral therapy), and caregiver support (e.g., multifamily groups). In its typical format with an adjunctive medical team, Psychoeducational Family Therapy is the treatment of choice for schizophrenia. It exemplifies the use of empirical data to design effective treatments where the nature of the illness shapes definitions of appropriate caregiving behavior. Thus, it has wide applicability for physiological and psychological disorders requiring high levels of family support such as Parkinson's disease and childhood asthma. There are multiple variants within Psychoeducational Family Therapy (e.g., Falloon, Boyd, & McGill, 1984; Goldstein, Rodnick, Evans, May, & Steinberg, 1978). Because Anderson, Reiss, and Hogarty (1986) have subsumed much of the earlier variants into a comprehensive approach, their model composes the focus of this chapter.

Although not a true variant of Psychoeducational Family Therapy, *Medical Family Therapy*, developed by McDaniel, Doherty, Rolland, and colleagues, promotes the role and value of the family therapist in the medical field (McDaniel, Hepworth, & Doherty, 1992; Rolland, 1994). These proponents have enumerated the need and advantages of having a family therapist as part of a medical team. This therapeutic utility is most credible during a crisis (e.g., diagnosis of terminal illness; suicide) or emergency (e.g., auto accident), or when a family needs help adjusting to the chronic illness of one of its members.

Basic Summary

Theory

- Symptoms reflect characteristics of the illness exacerbated by external stressors.
- Families do not cause schizophrenia but can enhance patient functioning by creating a low-stress home environment.

Therapy

- The goal of therapy is to delay relapse by helping the patient to slowly regain functioning.
- The model incorporates structural and behavioral techniques in conjunction with information about the illness.

Therapist

- The therapist is active and directive.
- The therapist serves as a liaison between the medical treatment team and the family.

Training

- Personal therapy is not required.
- Knowledge of the illness is essential.
- Supervision occurs through videotape, cotherapy, direct observation, and peer group consultation.

Origin and Evolution

Researchers have observed that schizophrenics released from inpatient facilities and returning home to emotionally charged families required readmittance sooner than patients from more tranquil families. Subsequent studies support this observation (Brown, Monck, Carstairs, & Wing, 1962, Brown, Birley, & Wing, 1972; replication by Vaughn & Leff, 1976; Vaughn, Snyder,

Jones, Freeman, & Falloon, 1984). Nine months after hospital release, patients whose families displayed high levels of expressed emotion (i.e., more negativity and invasiveness) had relapse rates of 50%—versus 13%–15% for low expressed emotion families. Interestingly, patients could reduce relapse rates even in high expressed emotion households if their face-to-face contact with family members was fewer than 35 hours per week, regardless of psychopharmacological compliance.

Other research has revealed two additional contexts that were detrimental to recently released schizophrenic patients: unstructured, confrontive, insight-based therapy, and highly active foster homes and day programs (Linn, Caffey, Klett, Hogarty, & Lamb, 1979; Linn, Klett, & Caffey, 1980). Anderson, Reiss, and Hogarty (1986) concluded that situations requiring adaptive responses to complex, ambiguous, or emotional stimuli elevate relapse rates, probably through physiological arousal. From this empirical work, a group of models emerged that viewed families as valued members of the treatment team, rather than an etiological source of the patient's illness.

☐ Key Terms

Expressed Emotion—the level of critical, hostile, or intrusive comments made by family members about the absent patient during a structured interview; an important predictor of functioning in schizophrenia and clinical depression, with higher levels associated with more relapse.

Diathesis-Stress Model—genetic predisposition determines risk for illnesses such as schizophrenia; among those at risk, environmental factors influence illness onset and progress.

Benign Indifference—a neutral style of interaction purposefully encouraged in family members; exposure to heightened emotion of either a positive or negative valence is difficult for schizophrenics to tolerate, increasing physiological arousal and symptom exacerbation.

☐ Key Techniques

Unique to this approach is the provision of disease-related information. During a one-day workshop, families receive facts about the illness, along with a critical message from the medical treatment team: they are not the cause of the patient's illness but a potentially powerful source of positive influence. Additionally, Psychoeducational Family Therapy adopts techniques from two other theories:

Structural Family Therapy

- joining with the patient and family to generate motivation (e.g., asking each member for his or her perspective of family functioning);
- strengthening individual and intergenerational boundaries (e.g., asking members to speak only for themselves, encouraging activities within specific subgroups);
- weakening rigid boundaries often existing between the family and the community (e.g., reducing isolation by encouraging attendance at multifamily support groups).

Behavioral Family Theory

- contingency contracting to set reasonable limits and enforce appropriate and consistent consequences;
- problem-solving and communication skills training (e.g., moderating conversational detail to reduce the patient's proneness to distraction);
- miscellaneous techniques such as shaping, extinction, positive reinforcement, modeling, and behavioral rehearsal.

☐ Basic Tenets

How Do Problems Arise?

Although schizophrenia has an unknown etiology, researchers generally accept a diathesis-stress explanation. Environmental factors affect onset among those individuals with a genetic predisposition toward the disorder. For example, stressful life circumstances such as moving away from home to attend college may be precipitating factors but only among those already at biological risk for schizophrenia. Accordingly, symptoms are products of the disease, and although influenced by environmental factors, they serve no function within the family system.

It is important to note that although theories of schizophrenia implicating the family as a causal agent fueled interest in the early field of MFT, no empirical support exists for once popular concepts such as Bowen's mother–child symbiosis or Bateson's double-bind. Yet the general observation that generated these theories is correct; families of schizophrenics are often different—socially isolated and overly involved with the patient. Such differences reflect rather than cause the illness, arising from social stigma and caregiving demands.

How Do Problems Persist?

Relapse is simply a feature of the illness. Highly negative or excessively intrusive environments, however, can accelerate the time to next relapse. Because these environments are difficult for the patient to tolerate, they cause physiological arousal and symptom exacerbation.

What Is the Objective of Therapy?

Therapy seeks not to eliminate but to postpone relapse. Postponement is a critical goal; with every relapse, patients typically experience increasingly severe decrements in functioning. The first year of release is particularly important; those patients able to manage symptoms well enough to avoid relapse during this time are at substantially reduced risk for subsequent hospitalization over the long term. Even in optimal environments, however, eventual relapse is likely.

What Produces Change?

Patients reduce risk for relapse when environments characterized by high expressed emotion become similar to low expressed emotion households—less negative and less organized around the illness. In addition, families must moderate displays of all emotions, including even positive but overly exuberant reactions. Excessive emotion in any form is potentially harmful to the patient's functioning.

How Does Change Occur?

Education about the illness normalizes the experience of families; blame and frustration shift away from the patient and toward the illness. Encouragement of nonfamilial social contact enhances coping and reduces social stigma. Therapy provides a sense of hope and emphasizes the maintenance of a neutral emotional climate, while encouraging reasonable limit setting and reshaping appropriate individual and intergenerational boundaries.

How Does Treatment Proceed?

Phase 1: Therapist tasks during the patient's hospital stay include the following steps:

- Establish a working alliance with the patient and family by
  - joining:
    - identifying benefits of participation for each member,
    - showing concern for family-related issues (e.g., question how siblings are faring through the crisis),
    - visiting briefly with the psychotic patient;
  - assessing stressors and available resources (e.g., recent unemployment, social support system);
  - emphasizing apparent strengths, problems avoided, and stamina required to handle the illness;
  - devising a contract containing mutual, attainable, and specific goals:
    - conveying minimal expectations through a year-long timeline,
    - concentrating initially on the patient's welfare,
    - using later sessions to address family concerns.

Phase 2: Medical treatment team tasks during the patient's hospital stay include the following tasks:

- Host a day-long workshop for multiple families
  - excluding patients to prevent overstimulation and allow members to discuss problems freely;
  - providing illness-related information to reduce anxiety, enhance adaptation, and prepare families for therapy sessions that follow the hospital release:
    - presenting general information (e.g., history, epidemiology, pharmacology),
    - describing typical (but inadequate) attempts to deal with the illness (e.g., rationalizing with the patient, attempting to interpret nonsensical statements),
    - explaining a diathesis-stress model of schizophrenia, with arousal from sources such as conflict increasing distraction, anxiety, and symptoms;
  - outlining the year-long treatment process:
    - maintaining a moderate level of patient stimulation,
    - setting a relaxed yet nonpermissive home environment,
    - helping the patient slowly return to a prior role within the family,
    - modulating family stress (i.e., decrease conflict, boundary ambiguities, simultaneous interactions, inconsistent rules),
    - developing an attitude of benign indifference (i.e., neutral affect);
  - preparing the family for the patient's release:

- ♦ identifying minimal rules that satisfy each member of the family (e.g., parents may tolerate what siblings cannot),
- ♦ sharing rules with the patient without detailed explanations, threats, or emotional displays,
- ♦ anticipating limit testing and apply consequences consistently,
- ♦ informing patients that some rules benefit the family (i.e., the patient is not always the center of attention),
- ♦ ignoring selective nontargeted problems except when involving abuse (e.g., may require police aid) or prodromal sources (i.e., subtle, idiosyncratic indications of decompensation requiring treatment);

- ➢ teaching communication skills training (e.g., avoid mindreading thereby forcing patient to convey ideas more clearly);
- ➢ encouraging hobbies and nonfamilial interests to enhance coping;
- ➢ offering multifamily support groups to decrease isolation and social stigma.

Phase 3: Therapist tasks during 6–12 months after hospital release include the following:

- meeting with the entire family or appropriate subgroups;
- spacing sessions at two-week intervals:
  - ➢ reinforcing the message of slow change,
  - ➢ allowing family to have access to the treatment team between sessions;
- following up on any previously assigned tasks:
  - ➢ emphasizing the importance of homework,
  - ➢ establishing continuity between sessions,
  - ➢ allowing for feedback.

Phase 4: Therapist tasks during 12–24 months after hospital release are as follows:

- focusing on social and work domains:
  - ➢ increasing contact with nonfamilial individuals slowly,
  - ➢ practicing school and vocationally related tasks;
- redirecting families who achieve the basic contract (i.e., patient operates at the level of functioning exhibited prior to illness onset):
  - ➢ offering families weekly sessions and renegotiating a new goal (e.g., resolve marital problems, examine family roles),
  - ➢ encouraging some form of long-term contact to maintain continuity.

What Is the Role of the Therapist?

Therapists represent simultaneous interests. When meeting with the family, they serve as staff representatives of the medical treatment team, providing information about hospital procedures and patient progress. When meeting with the medical treatment team, they represent the family, providing information about patient functioning and treatment concerns. Across settings, therapists are active and directive. For example, therapists control sessions by maintaining a focus on treatment goals, insisting on consistent attendance, and rescheduling sessions if patients and families are unwilling to stop inappropriate behavior (Anderson et al., 1986).

6

CHAPTER

Communication Models: Mental Research Institute

Overview

The Mental Research Institute (MRI) assumes that accumulated skills typically allow us to handle minor difficulties, daily hassles, and small problems. Then exceptions occur—the problem is too novel or the needed skills are not present. During these exceptions, successive unsuccessful attempts to fix the problem and reduce distress increase the likelihood of perpetuating the problem. The problem generates distress. And, in MRI, distress, not behavior, is the focus of therapy. MRI tries to lower distress (or remove the presenting problem) by having the client behave differently when the problem situation occurs. In general, treatment consists of assigning out-of-session tasks that increase behavior incompatible to the distress-producing behavior.

Basic Summary

Theory

- A problem, and the distress it produces, occurs when a smaller problem is mishandled, and the mishandling produces more distress.
- Once a problem occurs, attempted solutions to remedy the problem usually vary only slightly, in effect, doing more of the same. Doing more of the same makes the problem worse.

- Two factors maintain the problem after it starts:
  - inadequate solutions to the current and earlier versions of the problem; and
  - other people, usually family members, influence the attempted solutions.

Therapy

- The goal of therapy is to lessen the distress associated with the presenting problem. Distress is lessened by
  - removing or altering behaviors associated with the presenting problem, usually done with out-of-session tasks;
  - reframing the presenting problem in a way that makes it less distressing.

Therapist

- The therapist assesses how the client views the problem and reviews previous attempts to fix the problem.
- The therapist assigns tasks that alter the behavior or the perspective associated with the problem.
- The therapist conveys that the client must take behavioral action.

Training

- Personal therapy is not required.
- Consultation with peers is frequent.
- Live or videotaped supervision is common.
- Observation teams may be used.

Origin and Evolution

In 1959 Don Jackson started MRI in Palo Alto, California. Staffed by Jules Riskin and Virginia Satir, it began as a research project to study schizophrenics and their families. Paul Watzlawick joined the staff in 1961. During this period Gregory Bateson and his research team (Jay Haley, John Weakland, William Fry) were also in Palo Alto studying the communication patterns of schizophrenic families. Haley, Weakland, and Fry joined MRI after Bateson's project ended in 1962. Major staff changes occurred when Satir moved to the Esalen Institute in Big Sur, California, in 1966, and Haley went to the Philadelphia Child Guidance Clinic in 1967. Later additions to the MRI staff included Arthur Bodin, Richard Fisch, Lynn Segal, and Carlos Sluzki.

Theoretical Origins

During its early years, two distinct influences helped formulate MRI's theoretical premises: the interactional perspective (i.e., General Systems Theory) and practical therapy implementation (see Griffin, 1993). MRI theory was, and still is, invested intellectually in systems and cybernetic ideas. These ideas have at least six distinct sources:

General Systems Theory—An individual is part of a larger dynamic system that continuously evolves, adapts to environmental stimuli, and acts to preserve itself (von Bertalanffy, 1968).

Cybernetics—infused the mechanistic terms homeostasis, feedback loops, and information into General Systems Theory (Weiner, 1961).

Don Jackson—applied General Systems Theory and Cybernetics concepts as family interaction processes (e.g., homeostasis, feedback loops, equipotentiality, and equifinality). He also emphasized the cognitive and attributional features of communicative acts (Jackson, 1960, 1964; Watzlawick, Beavin, & Jackson, 1967).

Gregory Bateson—His work was used to help MRI develop an expansive theoretical base using tidbits of thinking and evidence from such diverse disciplines as anthropology, biology, and ethnology (Bateson, 1972, 1979). Bateson and colleagues proposed the double-bind theory of schizophrenia. According to the theory, the disease occurs when an individual continuously receives contradictory messages from family members and is unable to comment on or exit the predicament.

Paul Watzlawick—Following the scholarly approach established by Bateson, Watzlawick has continuously updated the thinking in MRI (Watzlawick, 1984, 1990). In particular, he has focused on the role of perception, attribution, and behavioral interaction as consequences of an individual's or group's assumptions about reality. More recently, Watzlawick has focused on second-order cybernetics and its assertion that the observer is a part of the observed system and, therefore, affects the system because of the observation.

Milton Erickson—infused indirect hypnosis techniques into MRI via Haley (Haley, 1963; 1973). While the Palo Alto group focused on the intricacies of communication, they depended on Erickson to illustrate how paradoxes, confusion, and other forms of communicative instructions are used as therapeutic tools.

As it evolved during the 1960s, MRI rejected the psychodynamic view that aberrant behavior reflects internal conflict; instead, it postulated that individuals are reactors to information via social interaction. Using this supposition as its foundation, MRI constructed a theory based on scientific ideas of behavior, not on metaphysical notions (e.g., the super ego; see Watzlawick, 1990). Because of the reactionary nature of the process, the novel thinking produced therapy suggestions that were radical for their time. MRI developed, for example, interpersonal and context-based interpretations of behavior, brief therapy, live supervision, and nonnormative assumptions about behavior. These concepts and training methods are now standard in most contemporary family therapy models.

The model has not changed much since the ideas were forwarded and techniques codified by Jackson and colleagues during the mid to late 1960s and by Watzlawick from the 1970s until the present. Several new variants of MRI are popular among family therapists. Most notable among the offspring are Solution Focused Therapy, Milan, and the Narrative or Externalization approach. These variants are discussed in more detail at the end of this chapter.

Key Terms

Reality—MRI maintains that, "All purposeful human behavior depends greatly on the views or premises people hold, which govern their interpretations of situations, events, and relationships" (Fisch, Weakland, & Segal, 1982, p. 5). From this perspective, reality is perception based, occurring as order is instilled on the continuous flow of experiences. Interpretation of reality depends on how and where the perceiver instills order. Two types of reality are posited from this constructivist position:

- *First order:* Objects exist outside of perception.
- *Second order:* Interpersonal interactions generate perceptions; in turn, these perceptions form an image of reality. Reality formed by construction is dynamic and evolves with information.

Normal Behavior—There is not necessarily a right or wrong way for an individual or family to behave. MRI does not intervene in an area unless an individual or family member has a complaint about the problem (Fisch et al., 1982).

Communication—the act of sending or receiving information.

- A person cannot not communicate.
- Every communication has a content and a relationship aspect; the latter classifies the former.
- The communicant's punctuation of the interaction determines the nature of a relationship (Watzlawick et al., 1967).
- There are two types of communication methods:
  - *Digital:* discrete sounds or utterances. Digital reflects the language (words) that represent some object, but the word itself is not like the object.
  - *Analogic:* the language of symbolic representation; analogic language, compared with digital, has object-like characteristics. Nonverbal behavior is analogic and it carries symbolism; the behavior represents its referent (Watzlawick et al., 1967). For example, a frown represents sadness. Nonverbal interactional behaviors define, and are symbolic of, the relationship among the interactants.

Relationship—A relationship is not an entity, it is an interaction with meanings associated with the ongoing behaviors. Relationships are either symmetrical or complementary.

- Symmetry implies equal, while complementary implies superior or inferior positions.
- Neither is better nor worse; they simply reflect patterns of interaction.

Quid pro quo—(if you do X, I will do Y) is the ground rule within the relationship.

- This exchange process is neither good nor bad but rather a by-product of system evolution.
- The behaviors exchanged through quid pro quo reflect agreements held by the interactants.
- Crisis occurs when the quid-pro-quo agreement changes without prior agreement between the individuals.

System—how one person engages another person defines the relationship between the two individuals; this process of creating a relationship is a system.

Circular Causality—behavior is simultaneously cause and effect. As noted by Wynne (1988), the term is inappropriate because of its temporal impossibility. However, it does convey appropriately the concept that a behavior can be both an antecedent and a consequence.

Family Homeostasis—the relative constancy of the system's steady state maintained by rule-regulated behavioral patterns.

Equifinality—different beginnings may produce similar outcomes; hence, input does not predetermine output, nor can one infer the input is based on output.

Equipotentiality—similar events (inputs) across individuals cannot be assumed to have similar effects (outputs). This concept is contrary to most popular "pop" psychology theories of cause and consequence (e.g., traumatic events or sexual abuse produce inevitable outcomes).

Change—altering behavior that is associated with the presenting problem; it has two types, as follows:

- *First order:* change that occurs within a system, yet the system itself remains unchanged. In many situations, first-order change is sufficient to remove the presenting problem.
- *Second order:* a change in the structure of the system forcing new rules and internal order (Watzlawick, Weakland, & Fisch, 1974).

Pars-pro-toto—literally means *parts can substitute for the whole.* Watzlawick (1978) discusses the concept of *pars-pro-toto* as a rationale for fixing a part, not the complete image, of the problem. He argues that understanding, handling, manipulating, and getting task compliance for a small portion of the problem is easier than dealing with the whole problem.

Customer or Window Shopper—Unique to this model is the explicit assessment of a client's willingness to change. Clients are classified as being either customers (i.e., those willing to work for change) or window shoppers. *Window shoppers* talk about changing but seem to be responding to pressure from others. They perceive the problem residing with someone else, or—if it is within their domain—it is a low magnitude problem and not worthy of a great deal of effort (i.e., insufficient distress). They express little investment in changing and will leave therapy when those individuals or institutions pressuring them have reduced the pressure. *Customers* are those individuals willing to change their behavior because either the problem is distressing enough or they simply want the change. This distinction is inherent in the MRI position because of a basic assumption: people will not change unless there is sufficient motivation—either because of distress or because of a genuine desire to alter their behavior.

☐ Key Techniques

Among family therapy orientations, MRI has the largest accumulation of behavior change techniques. Most of the techniques were derived from Erickson (see Haley, 1963, 1973) and given theoretical support through the writings of Watzlawick and colleagues (Bodin, 1981; Fisch et al., 1982; Watzlawick, 1976, 1978, 1990; Watzlawick et al., 1974). Some of the more popular techniques are as follows:

Reframing—The therapist changes "the conceptual and/or emotional setting or viewpoint in relation to which a situation is experienced and to place in another frame which fits the 'facts' . . . [and] thereby change[s] its entire meaning" (Watzlawick et al., 1974, p. 95). A reframe, unlike an interpretation, does not purport to uncover truth; instead, it attempts to alter the constructed image of the problem and the context within which it resides (Griffin, 1993; Watzlawick, 1978). Watzlawick (1978) reports that reframing was first described by Antiphon of Athens [480–411 B.C.]; thus the use of narrative and rhetoric to alter another's perspective is neither novel nor recent.

Utilizing Resistance—in situations where the client is not responding or changing only slightly to the task, the therapist asks that he or she slow down or, better yet, not change. This poses a dilemma to the client, complying with the therapist (i.e., not doing anything different) or not complying, which requires changing. This is similar to, although less focused than, "restraining change." (See Chapter 3, Strategic Family Therapy, Key Techniques.)

Utilizing the Devil's Pact—The therapist demands carte blanche (i.e., unconditional authority) before giving a task. For example, after a detailed discussion of the problem, the therapist might say, "I can fix X, but you have got to be willing to do everything I ask. If you do everything I ask, it will be solved; if not, the problem remains. What is your choice?"

Manipulating the Symptom—the therapist alters when, how, and where a symptom appears. Although each therapeutic maneuver manipulates the symptom differently, all permit the individual or system to view the seemingly omnipotent symptom as less powerful and, consequently, controllable and unnecessary.

- Advertising rather than concealing—calling attention to the symptom in situations where power or leverage derives from its concealment. After becoming public, its presence cannot be used as a reason to avoid action.
- Prescribing and scheduling the symptom—therapist prescribes when and where to exhibit the problem behavior. Compliance implies control of the symptom.
- Symptom practicing—client practices the behavior that characterizes the symptom; this practice implies the ability to control the symptom.
- Replacing the symptom—with another more beneficial one. A behavior similar to the symptom, yet somehow productive or beneficial, is prescribed for the client. Theoretically, then, the occurrence of the new behaviors allows a perspective shift toward the problem.

☐ Basic Tenets

How Do Problems Arise?

Attempting to fix small difficulties sometimes leads to larger problems. After initially failing to fix the problem, efforts are made to fix it in the same ways that were attempted in the past. This makes the problem worse. Three factors make this mishandling worse:

- Deny that there is a problem—no action is taken.
- Problem is either not solvable or nonexistent—unnecessary action is taken.
- Attempt a *first-order* change when only a *second-order* change will remove the problem (Bodin, 1981; see Key Terms).

Moreover, MRI views the presenting problem simply as distress of sufficient magnitude to justify the client coming to therapy. A presenting problem is not symptomatic of some larger, subsurface pathology. A problem is simply a problem—reflecting nothing more than the degree of distress exhibited by the client.

How Do Problems Persist?

Once established, interactional patterns among relevant individuals maintain the problem. Consistent with the notion that the problem is interpersonal, and not intrapsychic, each person has some part in perpetuating the behaviors necessary for the problem to be manifest. MRI wants to know how each person contributed to the ineffective prior attempts to remove distress.

What Is the Objective of Therapy?

The goal is to reduce distress by removing or reducing the problem by either changing interactions (i.e., making the problem nonexistent) or perceptions (i.e., viewing the problem as less distressing). Treatment addresses the following three general dimensions:

- What to change
  - ➢ Change in interactions alters or reduces the problem. Therapy instructs family members how to respond differently when the problem sequence begins. Instructions may be general to all family members or specific role changes to each family member.
  - ➢ Rather than redirect interaction patterns to reduce the negative behavior associated with distress, the task has two objectives:
    - ♦ increase incompatible positive behaviors, and
    - ♦ change relevant behavioral sequences in a way that makes the problematic behavior patterns unnecessary.
  - ➢ If the problem behavior does not change, then the objective is to alter, via perception change, the distress caused by the interactions.
- How much to change—Whether altering behaviors or perceptions, therapy changes only a portion of the problem (i.e., *pars-pro-toto*). Watzlawick argues that rather than fixing the big problem, some small component of the behavior should be modified—it is easier to comprehend and easier to get compliance from the client.
- Level of change—At the micro or proximal level, MRI changes behavior; at the system level, it changes rules. From their perspective, a system adapts to change because it has rules for changing rules; system rigidity reflects the lack of rules about handling change. When new behaviors occur in the system, there is a concomitant rule change. In addition, new rules improve the chances of the handling of future problems.

What Produces Change?

Change occurs when altering either perception or behavior reduces distress. Even if the behavior surrounding the problem does not change, and if by chance, or by therapy, the problem is perceived as less (or gone), a problem no longer exists.

How Does Change Occur?

MRI focuses on interaction patterns around the problem, specifically altering those associated with previous attempts to fix the problem. Intervention involves at least two people. Even with the intervention directed toward interactions, it can still be at the level of perception given the assumption that perception alters interaction.

How Does Treatment Proceed?

General Information

- *In-session change*—In-session therapy does not attempt to change behaviors; instead, it focuses on elucidating the processes that maintain the problem and developing solutions to alter the patterns.
- *Out-of-session change*—Out-of-session changes are necessary for this model to work. Strategies discussed in-session must be implemented between sessions. Results from the tasks are discussed during the next session and then new or modified tasks are assigned.

Initial Contact—The initial telephone conversation determines who is involved with the problem and who is calling relative to the problem; specifically,

- are they calling for someone else or
- do they have the problem.

Intake

- Participants—All pertinent individuals should attend the initial session. Each participant provides his or her perspective of the problem.
- Assessment—has two parts:
  - ➢ determining the parameters of the problem, and
  - ➢ determining the motivation of the client.

Problem Parameters—describe the role of the problem in the client's life. This information helps the therapist conceptualize the client's construction of the problem and is essential to developing an effective task. The parameters listed below are either overtly assessed with questions or indirectly determined through the client's general responses:

- What is the presenting problem? (That is, describe the complaint.)
- For whom is it a problem?
- How does the client think of the problem?

- Describe past efforts to fix the current complaint. (That is, what was the attempted solution?)
- How is the complaint causing distress (i.e., how is it a problem)?
- How does the problem change the behavior of the client—either by
  - ➢ avoiding doing something or
  - ➢ acting in a way that the individual does not like?
- What has occurred to make it a problem now?
- Is the client a customer?

Treatment

- How does the client think of treatment? For example, how should it occur; what should occur?
- What specifically does the client expect or want from treatment?
- How does the client view the problem, and how does that perspective influence the goals of therapy?
- Given the client's view of the problem, what expectations does the client have of the therapist?

Relevant Others

- The therapist determines exactly what brought the family into therapy:
  - ➢ does the IP want change,
  - ➢ does the family what change, and
  - ➢ are they in agreement about what change is desired and acceptable?
- How do other family members hold the client's view of the problem—different or similar?

Change

- Given what has been tried, what would a 180% attempted solution look like?
- What interaction patterns maintain the problem?
- What interaction patterns are impeding change?

The immediate section above describes general MRI therapy principles and concepts. Below is an outline of the therapy format for the Brief Therapy Center at Palo Alto. Unlike general MRI, its procedure is somewhat scripted, thus providing therapist guidelines for treatment structure (see Segal, 1991). The seven parts of the brief therapy format are listed below:

- Identify the family members most motivated for change and get them to the first session. However, in brief therapy the entire family is not needed, only the one with the perceived problem. This assumes that pattern alterations in behavior will permeate and modify system level interactions.

- Determine the exact nature of the problem—what, where, how, and who. Emphasis is on determining what interaction in the current environment maintains the displeasing behavior and how changes in the interaction will affect the presenting problem.
- Get consensus on a goal; it must be specific. The therapist determines the goal of therapy, while the model specifies how the goal can be achieved.
- From the goal, develop a plan to remove the problem. Since a logical fix is thought to be maintaining the distressing problem, to remove the problem the intervention should not be a logical "next-step." Watzlawick (1978) suggests that three things can be done to combat the "next-step" mentality:
  - use right-hemisphere (symbolic) language patterns;
  - block the left-hemisphere (logical) thinking; and
  - implement a specific behavioral prescription that is incompatible with the logical "next step."
- Assume that previous attempts to fix the problem currently maintain it; treatment seeks to interrupt the attempted solutions. Thus, all prescriptions for change require that the client do something different than was done before. New interactions should increase alternative, positive behavior rather than implement behaviors intended to reduce negative behaviors.
- Assess the effectiveness of the task. At each session, the client reports on the effectiveness of the previously assigned task. Using this information, the task (usually the same one or some variant) is modified to more effectively alter interactions.
- Terminate when the problem (or the distress it causes) lessens, even slightly, over an extended duration. When to terminate is well defined: when the problem is no longer a problem. This occurs when the client is less distressed with the problem or when there has been at least a small but significant change in the problem. If change maintains itself for at least several weeks and the client assumes that he or she can control those factors influencing the problem, then terminate. Since MRI is generally short term and problem focused, termination is the end stage of a normal process used to fix a problem. This implies that the client has shown the ability to use existing behavior change methods. In addition, the client can come back for help if new problems occur.

What Is the Role of the Therapist?

The therapist is responsible for changing the client's response to the distressing situation. In order to change behavior, the therapist may need to manipulate the person, situation, or both. MRI recognizes the therapist as a manipulator operating at two levels, the overt and the covert.

- At the overt level, the therapist seeks compliance to task assignments. The therapist uses any available tools—family members, teachers, employers, and even natural resistance to change—to get compliance.
- At the covert level, the therapist is continuously changing the client's perspective. Using abstractions and reframes, the therapist shifts the client's frame of reference about the problem and subtly encourages new ways of attacking the problem.

☐ Variants

This section reviews several family therapy models that derived, either directly or indirectly, from the writings of MRI. Some, like Milan, readily acknowledge this influence; others, like Narrative, show clear conceptual linkage to MRI but fail to acknowledge this influence. This section briefly describes the models, gives a few important points, and provides the essential references.

Milan Family Therapy (Systemic)

Basic Summary

Sometimes referred to as the systemic approach, the Milan model was influenced by the work of Bateson (1972) and MRI. Proponents consider it the purest family therapy adaptation of the systems' perspective. It attempts to alter dysfunctional family patterns by inducing second-order change (system level) via circular questioning, positive connotations, and behavior change task assignments (e.g., rituals, prescriptions). Milan moved from using paradoxical interventions to giving invariant prescriptions and, more recently, to variant prescriptions (tailored to the family). In the last two decades, the systemic approach has undergone several major personnel and theoretical shifts. In the personnel area, Mara Selvini-Palazzoli and Guiliana Prata split from Luigi Boscolo and Gianfranco Cecchin, each group forming a unique treatment and training facility.

As noted, Milan has undergone numerous changes since its inception. These changes occurred roughly over three periods.

- Early Milan used paradoxical injunctions to alter interaction patterns.
- Middle Milan used an invariant prescription (i.e., the task was the same for all families irrespective of symptom):
  - ➢ parents record family members' reactions after being told that the parents have a secret;

  - ➢ eventually parents secretly disappear from the home for varying lengths of time;
  - ➢ reactions to the secret and the sojourns generate information for the sessions (Selvini-Palazzoli approach).
- Recent Milan uses prescriptions that vary by family and problem (i.e., Selvini-Palazzoli approach). Alternatively, the Boscolo and Cecchin approach assumes that the therapy questioning process is the change agent. Their questions magnify differences among family members in the perception of the problem. This emphasis reflects the assumption that the recognition of differences alters perceptions, moving family members toward an integrative or systemic perspective.

This once influential model is used rarely today because of the personnel splitting and constantly shifting treatment format.

Important Contributions

Although not as popular or widely used as it once was, the Systemic Family Therapy model developed numerous terms and techniques found in many current models. For example:

Positive Connotation

- reframes the symptom so that it appears to serve a positive function within the family;
- all family behaviors, including the symptom, are considered important to the well-being and cohesion of the family and each of its members.

Therapeutic Rituals

- involve all family members and provide clarity of family relationships, both within and across generational boundaries;
- are framed as experiments, prescribing a time and place for the behavior to occur; it is sometimes used to exaggerate family rules or myths;
- are used to accentuate the positive connotation that has been constructed to explain the symptom.

Circular Questions

- gather information, generate hypotheses, and alter the family's perspective of the family (Tomm, 1984a, 1984b, 1988);

- address differences in perception by different family members;
- punctuate family processes, assuming that the punctuation creates system feedback and establishes a method for change.

General Assumptions

Milan holds numerous, clearly articulated assumptions about symptoms, family dynamics, and change. For example, it makes the following assumptions:

- The behavior of every family member serves to maintain the system in a homeostatic state.
- In the dysfunctional family, rules governing the system are too rigid; thus treatment seeks to induce flexibility into the system and broaden the range of acceptable behaviors.
- The problem's construction is family dependent, and the system collectively defines the problem. In effect, the problem creates a unique system. (Note: this position is similar to, but preceded the Narrative approach; in response to this assumption, Narrative seeks to externalize the problem.)
- The prescriptive intervention is
  - ➢ tailored to change the rules of the family system by focusing on changing the primitive, underlying myth that regulates the system;
  - ➢ delivered as a opinion or request for behavior change that should be done between sessions.
- Symptoms reflecting the game played by family members serve a function within the dysfunctional family system—the cost is a sacrificed family member. Yet the family's behavior is appropriate considering its conceptual configuration of the problem.
- No specific behavioral goals are negotiated with the family; change occurs randomly as information is added to the system via questions and rituals.
- Symptom alleviation follows interaction changes brought about by therapeutic rituals or prescriptions and in-session questions; it occurs over time as second-order change reflects the system's incorporation and accommodation to new information.
- The objective of treatment is to introduce information into the system to alter family rules, games, or myths, and consequently change the role of the symptom in the family.
- If a system component changes, the entire system must change; there cannot be a modification in one aspect of a system without changes in the entire system.

Therapy Implementation

The Milan model is a team approach and, for the most part, follows a standard procedure. A brief description follows:

- Treatment lasts about 10 sessions.
- Sessions are scheduled about 4–6 weeks apart.
- Male and female cotherapists are used:
  - ➢ another therapy team observes;
  - ➢ the therapy team behind the glass is used strategically to
    - ♦ offer opinions,
    - ♦ make suggestions, or disagree with the cotherapist team.
- Prescriptions are given, but the family is asked not to change for the time being.
- The main intervention is usually a ritual or positive connotation.
- A standard session is divided into five parts (see Tomm, 1984b):
  - ➢ Presession (5–20 min.): Team develops initial hypotheses about the family's functioning, and symptom formation.
  - ➢ Session (15–20 min.): Therapist interviews the family while the team observes; the team uses this time to validate, modify, or change hypotheses.
  - ➢ Intersession (15–30 min.): Team meets to discuss the hypotheses, the family, and the session. They construct an intervention.
  - ➢ Intervention (5–15 min.): Therapist delivers the intervention. Typically, interventions occur by positively connoting the problem situation or by asking the family to do a ritual. Prescribed rituals, like positive connotations, always comment on the problem situation.
  - ➢ Postsession (5–15 min.): Team discusses the intervention and the family's reaction to the intervention and develops a preliminary plan for the next session.

Role of the Therapist

The Milan therapist has a unique purpose in this model. He or she is usually part of a cotherapy team that, in turn, is part of a larger observation team. Important assumptions about the therapist are as follows:

- The therapist maintains a neutral stance: neutrality provides the family nothing to react against. Within this sphere of neutrality, the therapist asks circular questions and comments on observations and conveys hypotheses from the therapy team.

- The therapist, with the help of the team, comes to session with hypotheses that are forwarded via the circular questioning during the session; hypotheses are modified as the family reacts to the circular questioning.
- The objective is not to help the family change but instead to activate the family's inherent capacity to generate its own solutions (Boscolo, Cecchin, Hoffman, & Penn, 1987).

Narrative Family Therapy

Overview

Michael White and David Epston have developed a form of therapy that shifts the family's thinking from within the individual to outside the family, and from the family fearing the problem to being a united front against an outside entity. This externalization and problem manipulation process occurs using oral and written narratives, contracts, and certificates of achievement.

Key Term

Unique Outcomes—occasions when the problem did not occur, although the likelihood was high that it should have occurred. Similar to de Shazer's *exceptions* (de Shazer, 1985, 1988; see the following Solution Focused Therapy section).

Key Techniques

Questions—Using questions, the therapist directs the family to address how the problem has affected their lives and then to consider how family members have influenced the problem.

Externalization and Stories—Families are encouraged to reconstruct the problem as an outside entity, to observe and label its attributes, and then fight against its character. For example, a story often used to illustrate this method involves the encopretic child Nick and *Sneaky Poo*. Sneaky Poo became the personification of the encopresses, and Nick and his family constantly struggle with Sneaky Poo.

Basic Tenets and Therapy Outline

This therapeutic approach is influenced, although not acknowledged, by MRI-type thinking and strategic moves associated with Haley and Erickson (Haley, 1973). An additional influence is the work of Michel Foucault and his views on social oppression (see Fish, 1993). Using these perspectives of people, problems, and change as guidelines, White and Epston (1990) have outlined the process of change.

First, White and Epston see a family's struggle with a problem as analogous to some group of people being a victim of an oppressor (i.e., Foucault influence). The family is a victim to the problem. It oppresses the family, and the family can see it in no other frame of reference.

Second, White and Epston provide the family a new frame of reference to the problem. This is not drastically different from other forms of brief therapy that provide reframes either about the problem or the family's perception of the problem (e.g., MRI, Strategic). The difference is the systematic and strategic placement of the reframe. Families are convinced that the problem is an external entity worthy of a good struggle. Therapy then becomes a series of directed questions or comments about the struggle.

Finally, questions and comments direct the family toward times that they have won the battle with the problem. These are *unique outcomes*. Acknowledging these unique outcomes forces the family to question the omnipotence of the problem and provides strategies for defeating the problem. After the omnipotence is questioned, therapy becomes a series of opportunities via stories, letters, and certificates for the family to reconceptualize the problem in a way that the problem is either defeated or is no longer oppressive.

Solution Focused Therapy

Summary

This model began in the late 1970s in Milwaukee's Brief Family Therapy Center. Among the handful of names associated with this model (e.g., Bill O'Hanlon, Insoo Berg, Scott Miller, Michele Weiner-Davis), Steve de Shazer is the most prominent. He brings to Solution Focused Therapy MRI's thinking about utilizing the client's perspective and assumptions about reality and Ericksonian techniques for intervention. Therapeutic efforts are toward altering perceptions, increasing behavioral exceptions, and instilling a sense of competency in the client.

Proponents of Solution Focused Therapy argue that the biggest difference between this model and other brief therapies is the emphasis on finding solutions rather than focusing on problem construction and definition. Solution Focused advocates argue that, unlike other forms of family therapy, this model does not try to answer why a problem exists or how it began. This contention is somewhat contrived. No major brief therapies try to determine a specific etiological agent—all focus on the present, and all focus on behavior sequences that alter the outcome. In this sense, all focus on solutions.

In practice, the biggest difference between Solution Focused and other brief therapies is the time spent determining the parameters of the problem (e.g., where, when). While other models need to know specifics in order to construct effective tasks, Solution Focused primarily wants to know when the problem did not occur (i.e., exceptions); they then try to increase those situations. Assuming the therapist needs minimal information to construct an effective intervention, Solution Focused is similar to the position held by Erickson (Haley, 1973) and proponents of Neurolinguistic Programming (e.g., Bandler & Grinder, 1979).

Key Techniques

There are three major techniques associated with this approach:

Exceptions—The therapists wants to know when the problem did not occur or was not as bad; these are interpreted as opportunities to illustrate, define, and encourage the continuance of these exceptions (see also Unique Outcomes, Narrative Family Therapy, this chapter).

Miracle Question—The therapist poses the question, "Suppose that one night there is a miracle and while you were sleeping, the problem that brought you to therapy is solved: How would you know? What would be different?" Derived from an Ericksonian time progression technique, these questions are used to help the client and therapist decide

- what perceived differences need to occur to lessen the problem, and
- what will be the goal of therapy.

Scaling—The therapist attempts to quantify needed, desired, or current levels of behavior. To quantify means to assign a numeric value (e.g., 1–10) or set of values to some dimension of the problem. This allows the client and therapist to gauge how much change is expected or needed. For example, if a client reports being a 7 on depression, the therapist can ask how he would act differently if he were a 5 (improvement). This process of quantification, at least theoretically, increases the therapist's ability to externalize and modify behavior.

Several important suppositions underlie this model. First, drawn from the ideas expressed by Erickson (Haley, 1967), Solution Focused Therapy assumes that the client has the capacity to stop the problem. The job of the therapist is to use the client's existing resources, remove impediments to change, and help the client develop ways of allowing the desired behavior to occur. Another supposition, a variant of MRI's *pars-pro-toto* (see Chapter 6, MRI; Key Terms), states that the entire problem does not need to be modified, only some small portion of it. Like MRI, the Solution Focused model assumes that a small change is easier to implement than a large change and that a small change can lead to larger changes.

The popularity of this model has increased greatly during the last decade. With its theoretical clarity and lineage and its emphasis on treatment brevity, it is widely used in managed care mental health systems.

PART

II

HISTORICAL MODELS

7

CHAPTER

Object Relations Theory

Overview

Object relations theorists propose that the infant's contact with an early caregiver exerts profound life-long influence on subsequent interpersonal relationships. In effect, unconscious forces from childhood determine the behavioral patterns in current relationships. When early experiences are negative, pathological intrapsychic structures and processes result. Views of reality distort; individuals react unconsciously to images of the past rather than from current information. Thus, intrapsychic pathology commonly appears as relationship distress. Across multiple models within this approach, therapists typically intervene by identifying the individual unconscious processes inherent in current interaction and by offering aptly timed interpretations so that members achieve insight into problems and learn new ways of interacting. More recent extensions of this approach include work by David and Jill Scharff, David Schnarch, and Judith Siegel. This chapter concludes with an overview of these variants. Also, during the last 10–15 years several individually trained and oriented therapists have integrated psychodynamic precepts with systems assumptions. These are usually referred to as some form of integrative therapy (see, e.g., Nichols (1996) or Pinsof (1995)). Conversely, others therapists have moved from a traditional family systems approach to one viewing the individual as the system, exemplified by Schwartz's (1994) Internal Family Systems Therapy. His work appears as a variant at the conclusion of this chapter.

Basic Summary

Theory

- Early childhood trauma causes defective internal structures and processes.
- Relational problems indicate intrapsychic deficits.

Therapy

- The goal of therapy is to achieve an integrated view of reality through accepting repressed and forgotten memories.
- The therapist uses empathetic listening and insightful interpretations to access the latent meaning behind attitudes, motives, and behavior.

Therapist

- The therapist is nondirective.
- The therapist monitors personal intrapsychic processes to assess clients.

Training

- Personal therapy is a critical prerequisite to practice.
- Prior training in ahistorical models may hinder progress.
- Supervision involves analyzing internal reactions to clients.

Origin and Evolution

Most forms of Object Relations credit several sources of theoretical development. Melanie Klein was a British psychiatrist who received analysis from one of Freud's pupils. She believed that early experiences with the mother provide offspring with a lifelong template for all other relationships. Klein was also among the first theorists to introduce the concept of introject (i.e., internalized images of self and others). The British psychoanalyst, Ronald Fairbairn, elaborated on the influence of early experiences. He proposed that individuals reduce anxiety resulting from dependency during infancy by splitting the caregiver into three mental representations or objects: the ideal (comforting), the exciting (unsatiated), and the rejecting (hostile). Work by a later theorist, Donald Winnicot, extended these ideas; parenting that fails to achieve a minimally sufficient or "good enough" level of care causes excessive splitting early in life and prevents successful integration of internal objects in adulthood. Bad objects consume psychic energy needed by the central ego for evaluating reality and forming external relationships.

H. V. Dicks, a British psychoanalyst who established the Family Psychiatric Unit at the Tavistock Clinic in England, extended Fairbairn's psychology of the individual to marital dyads. Dicks identified marriage as the context for reliving original parenting experiences; marital distress arises from unconscious pathological levels of internal, unconscious processes (i.e., splitting and projective identification).

☐ Key Terms

Introject—repressed memories of early caregivers that reflect reality and fantasy; these mental images influence views of self and others.

- If earlier caregivers provided insufficient parenting, negative experiences become part of how offspring view themselves and others (i.e., internalized).
  - ➢ Internalized aspects remain unconscious.
  - ➢ Behavior and affect associated with insufficient parenting (e.g., inconsistency, anger) manifest later in how individuals relate to partners and raise children.
- The presence of introjects is inferred from behavioral and affective cues.

Splitting—a basic coping mechanism to reduce anxiety by isolating and repressing undesirable features of the caregiver. There are two possible outcomes with this mechanism:

- Termination by age two for those receiving sufficient early care; such individuals have achieved "object relations constancy":
  - ➢ acceptance of the caregiver's good and bad aspects,
  - ➢ emergence of a unified representation of reality containing good and bad,
  - ➢ generalization to accepting good and bad aspects of self and others.
- Perpetuation into adulthood for those receiving insufficient early care; such individuals are unable to achieve object relations constancy:
  - ➢ repression of the excessively negative qualities of the early caregiver,
  - ➢ emergence of a distorted view of reality wherein bad qualities of self are isolated and repressed.

Projective Identification—the unconscious process by which a mate or offspring unwittingly assumes another person's undesirable internalized features; negative aspects of the self are denied and assigned to others.

- This process occurs as follows (Ogden, 1982):
  - ➢ an unconscious desire to rid the self of bad or threatening qualities,

- ➢ subtle interactional cues to elicit these aspects in another,
- ➢ unwitting "collusion" by the target to adapt these aspects.
- Projective identification is unproblematic when occurring at low levels of psychopathology (e.g., compatibility in repressed aspects of the psyche produces marital satisfaction (Scharff & Scharff, 1991)).

Holding Environment—a setting where clients feel protected and safe because the therapist permissively accepts any free associations or spontaneous interactions. This context allows clients to

- access repressed or forgotten material needed for assessment,
- accept therapeutic interpretations as accurate,
- build respective holding environments within their own familial relationships.

Boundaries—the level of perceived differentiation between members in the couple or family (Siegel, 1992). Insufficient or diffuse boundaries:

- create inaccurate individual assessment of abilities and characteristics (i.e., low sense of self),
- elevate risk for being overinvolved in the lives of others.

Transference—the client's emotional reactions are overlayed onto other family members or the therapist; these reactions reflect early family relations instead of the current relationship. For example, a male therapist may consciously or unconsciously remind the client of his or her father; the client begins reacting to the therapist as if this were true.

Derivatives—the latent meaning behind attitudes, behaviors, or feelings; this is detected by therapists through analyzing personal reactions to session material.

☐ Key Techniques

Object Relations Theory deemphasizes techniques, instead focusing on building a sound therapist–patient relationship through empathic listening and insightful interpretation. Assessment follows from the analysis of countertransference phenomena.

Empathic Listening—concerted attention to detect the latent meaning behind speech or interactions; also conveys acceptance and understanding of the client. If skillfully done, it creates a therapeutic bond that paves the way for establishing a holding environment.

- A common strategy involves emotional linking (i.e., acknowledging the affective messages embedded in the client's speech).
- Cashdon (1988) provides an example: a client reports needing to exercise caution when discussing sensitive topics at work; the therapist labels it as depressing when coworkers are untrustworthy.

Interpretation—Therapists offer the subjective meaning or motive behind behavior, affect, or opinions.

- A common strategy involves linking current responses to the past.
  - "When in the past have you felt as angry as you are now with your spouse?"
  - "What early memories do you have about crying as hard as you are now?"
- Siegel (1992) thinks that these kinds of interpretations allow clients to connect current problems to causal events from the past.

Countertransference—the therapist's use of self (Siegel, 1992) or analysis of spontaneous reactions toward a client's transference phenomena; a vital source of information about intrapsychic deficits.

- Reactions to clients include
  - vague uneasiness,
  - anger or irritation,
  - doubts about therapeutic competence,
  - an inability to dismiss a song from awareness,
  - sexual attraction to the client.
- Constitutes a natural part of object relations therapy (Cashdon, 1988).
- Provides the basis of assessing the client's inner psyche (Siegel, 1992).

☐ Basic Tenets

How Do Problems Arise?

Problems reflect intrapsychic deficits in one or more family members. These deficits originate in early childhood trauma and typically involve inadequate parenting. Members with a deficit split or isolate these qualities and then projectively identify or elicit these aspects in other family members. This process reduces anxiety in the person with the deficit and provides a means for mastering the negative qualities (i.e., fighting them in another person). Accordingly, the symptom bearer may not be the person with the intrapsychic problem. Because symptoms can change shape within the current member, or even shift between members, amelioration receives less attention than attempts to resolve intrapsychic deficit.

How Do Problems Persist?

Problems persist because families are involved in a process of unconscious collusion in perpetuating the projective identification process. Collusion temporarily

- reduces anxiety in the person with the intrapsychic deficit,
- maintains self-esteem in the symptom bearer who serves a central role in the family,
- promotes cohesion within the family by providing a common concern or focus.

What Is the Objective of Therapy?

Therapists seek to improve intrapsychic functioning through having their clients release and accept repressed or forgotten material; family members can then react to one another based on current reality rather than images of the past. Problematic interactions will cease because projective identification processes become unnecessary to maintain intrapsychic equilibrium.

What Produces Change?

At a fundamental level, achievement of whole object relations occurs with the integration of good and bad objects. Individuals then have sufficient levels of intrapsychic strength to handle disappointments or setbacks. In other words, individuals who successfully resolve splitting become more balanced and realistic in their perceptions of others and more optimistic about the future.

How Does Change Occur?

Insight is a necessary but insufficient prerequisite for change. Family members must realize the influence that unconscious processes have in their lives and learn to accept their own negative aspects. Individuals must process the insight, meaning that the information produces an outward and desirable manifestation in the client's life. Often clients must relive and mourn unfulfilling aspects of past relationships, thereby garnering significant relief from insufficient parenting received during childhood.

How Does Treatment Proceed?

Therapy encompasses two phases:

- Short-term crisis intervention
  - ➢ reducing symptoms through clarifying communication and listening with empathy,
  - ➢ leaving any defenses intact (e.g., projective identification),
  - ➢ offering long-term reconstructive therapy upon achieving symptom reduction,
  - ➢ supporting families who desire only symptom relief in termination.
- Long-term intrapsychic reconstruction
  - ➢ deepening the holding environment by getting members to listen and understand without defensiveness;
  - ➢ using a nondirective manner to gather information about each member's past;
  - ➢ observing spontaneous interactions and free associations for derivatives;
  - ➢ eliciting material about early childhood memories:
    - ♦ parent–child interactions,
    - ♦ quality of care received;
  - ➢ monitoring personal internal process (e.g., emotional reactions, fleeting thoughts);
  - ➢ allowing emotional reactions to intensify as families become more comfortable with accessing repressed and forgotten material;
  - ➢ using in-session observations and countertransference to link current with historical functioning;
  - ➢ offering interpretations and examining any resistance;
  - ➢ terminating when clients accept and integrate interpretations, as evidenced by outward change.

What Is the Role of the Therapist?

Therapists generally assume a nondirective stance; they concentrate on encouraging members to speak freely and interact spontaneously. Interruptions, reassurance, advice, or guidance constitutes unnecessary interference. When asked, questions must not change the direction of the ongoing interaction but elicit clarification or amplification and typically highlight the underlying assumptions or projections ("What would your mother's reaction have been to Johnny's problem?"). Therapists offer interpretations designed to generate new discussions by revealing hidden motivations or avoided emotions.

Prior psychoanalytic training comprises the "single greatest asset" for becoming an object relations therapist (Scharff & Scharff, 1987, p. 29); such training yields skills on working with projective identification processes and countertransference phenomena. The authors warn that initial training in theories such as structural may hinder subsequent attempts to learn object relations because of intolerance for the latter's inherent ambiguity and difficulty in following rather than leading.

☐ Variants

Scharff and Scharff

The adult sexual relationship encapsulates the history of earlier relationships: sexual genitalia compose a projection screen of sorts for intrapsychic deficits (Scharff & Scharff, 1991). Treatment focuses on sexual functioning as an avenue for assessment and intervention, irrespective of the presenting problem. Therapists analyze fantasies and dreams; work with families includes play therapy (Scharff & Scharff, 1987).

Schnarch

Treatment follows the assumption that marital sexuality is the single greatest tool for human development (Schnarch, 1991). Couples come together in a crucible of intimacy, where intrapsychic deficits prevent achievement of full sexual potential (i.e., "wall-socket" sex—the unanticipated energy generated by an erotic connection). Therapists work with each partner to validate perspectives, promote personal integrity, and analyze intrapsychic processes.

Siegel

Marital distress stems from intrapsychic deficits that allow projective identification sequences to escalate (Siegel, 1992). Treatment combines communications skills training and intrapsychic analysis. Therapists correct distortions in communication through teaching clients to express affect in a neutral way. They also help the listener identify unrelated reactions to the partner's speech (i.e., individual projective identification process) that interfere with interpretation.

Schwartz

The mind is composed of a cluster of subpersonalities, each of which handles various tasks (Schwartz, 1994). With unresolved trauma, the "self" is unable to balance this internal system. Exiles (i.e., those parts composing the trauma experience) seek comfort but are suppressed by managers (i.e., overseers of daily tasks) that sometimes receive assistance from firefighters (i.e., interveners whose solutions often create further problems such as alcoholism). Therapists help the clients regain control or the parts so that the exiles can share and integrate trauma with other parts.

8

CHAPTER

Bowen Systems Therapy

Overview

Bowen Systems Therapy posits that individuals face a fundamental tension—attempting to satisfy opposing needs for familial connection and personal autonomy. Those who successfully balance these needs are rational and objective and are able to relate well to members of their nuclear and extended families. Individuals unable to achieve this balance react to momentary emotion; family contact is excessive or nonexistent. Such problems compose the cumulative effects of inadequate functioning across parents' and grandparents' generations. Therapists help clients identify the multigenerational family dynamics that cause the emotional illness, devise strategies for becoming more objective and less reactive, and implement change in nuclear and extended families. Two contemporaries of Bowen shared his belief that previous generations influence current functioning: Ivan Boszormenyi-Nagy and James Framo. This chapter concludes with a brief summary of their contributions to the multigenerational approach.

Basic Summary

Theory

- Emotional illness reflects the cumulative effects of functioning across three generations.

- As inherently unstable subsystems, dyads may seek relief by involving a third party in their interaction (i.e., triangulation).
- Triangulation of children causes them to exhibit emotional illness that persists into adulthood.

Therapy

- The goal of therapy is to separate intellectual from emotional functioning within the individual.
- The therapist works to extend intraindividual improvements to nuclear and extended family systems.

Therapist

- The therapist acts as a coach or consultant.
- The therapist stabilizes the marital dyad by becoming the third member.

Training

- Level of self-differentiation determines relative skill.
- Personal therapy is a critical prerequisite to practice.
- Supervision involves videotape review to assess the therapist's level of differentiation with the couple.

Origin and Evolution

As a psychoanalytically trained psychiatrist, Murray Bowen studied schizophrenia via mothers and children while at the Menninger Clinic from 1946 to 1954. He noticed their oscillating patterning of closeness and distance, a process he called mother–child symbiosis. This process seemingly captured an anxious attachment style in the mother that Bowen thought transferred to offspring as schizophrenia. Bowen continued this line of research, serving as the first director of the Family Division in the National Institutes of Mental Health until 1959; while there, he studied how fathers stabilized the mother–child dyad through triangulation. He often had the entire family hospitalized to allow for detailed observation and research. Bowen eventually incorporated influences from sibling and extended family into the dysfunctional interactions of parents and the symptomatic child. Later in the Department of Psychiatry at Georgetown University, he became involved extensively in the training of psychiatrists and other mental health professionals, until his death in 1990. Bowen has had wide influence in the field of family therapy, with many advocates, including Philip Guerin, Thomas Fogarty, Betty Carter, and Monica McGoldrick. More recently, adaptations of Bowen's theory augment generational influences with gender as another fundamental organizing principle in families (Carter & McGoldrick, 1988). Concern for the inherent social inequities of culturally prescribed gender roles has also produced an overarching perspective that promotes awareness of cultural biases across all theories (see Chapter 11).

Key Terms

Differentiation of Self—emotional detachment or the ability to maintain objectivity by separating affect from cognition. Emotionally detached individuals

- transcend individual and familial emotions;
- use personal principles as a guide;
- evidence adaptation and independence in family relationships;
- possess a solid or genuine self
  - less susceptible to influence by others,
  - more consistent in decisions across time.

Emotional Fusion—the inability to separate emotions from cognition; this is the opposite end of the continuum for emotional detachment. Emotionally fused individuals

- come from undifferentiated families;
- use emotions of self and others as a guide;
- evidence dependency or distance within familial relationships;
- possess a pseudo or false self
  - unaware of their own *ingenuineness*,
  - unable to take an I-position (see Key Techniques).

Emotional Cutoff—extreme forms of distancing between members in emotionally fused families; undifferentiated members withdraw physically or emotionally to cope with anxiety inherent in the defective system. Disadvantages include

- replication across generations,
- reduction in support available to the nuclear family.

Triangle—a three-member subsystem representing the smallest stable unit within the family; reduces dyad instability by using a third person to distract or ally with one of the members.

Nuclear Family Emotional Process—four relationship strategies used by spouses to handle anxiety; normative if constrained to transitory stressors:

- emotional distance: ignore one another or avoid discussing conflictual topics;
- marital conflict: create and maintain extremely intense arguments;
- spousal dysfunction: assume complementary roles as overfunctioner (i.e., "healthy") and underfunctioner (i.e., "ill");
- child dysfunction: draw a child into the interaction (i.e., triangulate) and cause a symptom to manifest in the offspring.

Family Projection Process—the process by which spiraling levels of emotional illness transmit across successive generations through the child dysfunction strategy.

- Emotional fusion creates anxiety between the spouses.
- Some parents seek stability and support from offspring to decrease anxiety within the marital dyad.
- Children react to these developmentally inappropriate demands by becoming unstable and anxious.
- Parents perceive problems as deficits of the child not the environment.
- A triangle forms:
  - ➢ one parent becomes overly solicitous toward the child;
  - ➢ the other parent mimics their partner's behavior or becomes distant.
- The triangulated child experiences problems in adulthood:
  - ➢ level of self-differentiation is lower than that of the parents;
  - ➢ marriage will be to someone of comparable dysfunction;
  - ➢ the child dysfunction strategy will likely surface in the new family.
- If the child dysfunction strategy replicates across successive generations (i.e., multigenerational transmission process), eventually a schizophrenic member will emerge.

Sibling Position—birth order within the nuclear family; shapes personality and familial role.

- Influence stems from functional rather than chronological position (e.g., a lone daughter in a family of sons may be a middle child based on her chronological age but receive treatment as the youngest because of her respective gender (Hall, 1983)).

- Oldest or youngest child roles are more vulnerable to triangulation.
- Roles become exaggerated and dysfunctional to the degree that the system is emotionally fused.

Key Techniques

This approach generally deemphasizes techniques. Instead, primary tools involve qualities of the self, as determined directly by the therapist's own level of self-differentiation.

Genograms—a diagram of the family's genealogy typically depicting three generations; presents problems as intergenerational in origin and organizes background information for assessment. Figure 2 contains examples of the diagrams used in genograms.

- Reveals nodal events:
  - ➢ significant milestones that unleash related changes;
  - ➢ possible replication across generations (e.g., father's sister dies in childhood at age 12; his own daughter develops problems at age 12 because the chronological event triggered unresolved issues of the earlier death in the father).
- Indicates level of adaptive functioning available.
- Organizes various forms of data:
  - ➢ births, abortions, miscarriages, deaths;
  - ➢ marriages, divorces;
  - ➢ geographic location;
  - ➢ frequency, mode of contact;
  - ➢ type of employment;
  - ➢ religious affiliation;
  - ➢ cultural, ethnic identity.

Going Home Task—clients establish contact with their family of origin to learn how members maintain emotional fusion; introduced as clients show improved self-differentiation.

I-Position—requests or statements that emphasize the speaker's personal responsibility for attitudes, behavior, or affect; enhances objectivity because the speaker refrains from blame. For example, "I get angry when you . . ." meets this structural requirement; "you make me angry . . ." does not. Therapists use this format to coach clients; clients practice these kinds of statements in session.

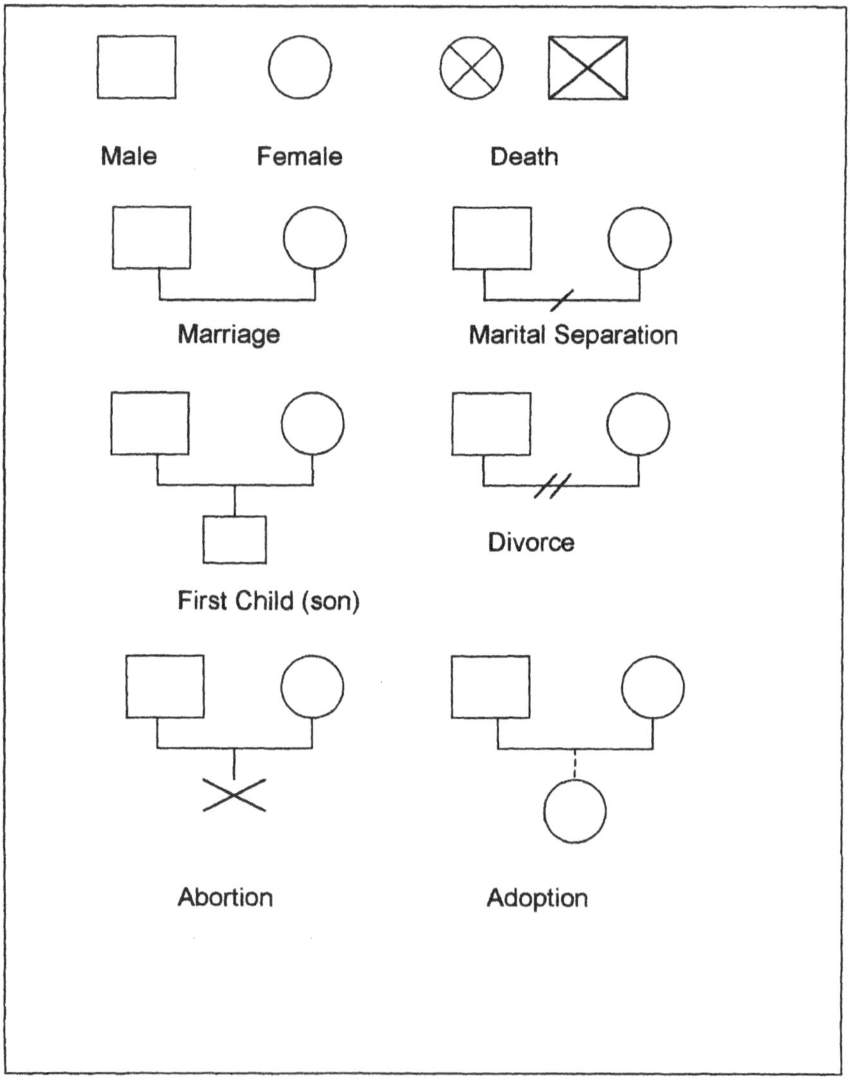

FIGURE 2. Symbols associated with Bowenian Family Therapy.

Basic Tenets

How Do Problems Arise?

All individuals display symptoms under sufficient levels of situational or chronic stress. Moreover, even differentiated individuals use strategies within the family projection process to reduce anxiety during stressful times. Emotionally fused individuals experience more symptoms over longer durations than differentiated counterparts largely because the former have fewer strategies for handling stressors (e.g., less adaptive coping skills).

How Do Problems Persist?

Problems are inherent to the family projection process (i.e., emotional distance, marital conflict, spousal dysfunction, and child dysfunction). Each strategy provides temporary relief—all a differentiated family needs—short-term solutions to transitory stressors. Marital conflict, for example, may temporarily stabilize the dyad; spouses argue and feel calmer afterward. Families of emotionally fused individuals experience anxiety not only from transitory sources but also from the defective system itself. With higher levels of anxiety, these families come to prefer a particular strategy, which, with overuse, loses effectiveness. For example, spouses who overuse marital conflict may experience fewer periods of relative calm because of residual anger and resentment. Key differences also arise in the use of the child dysfunction strategy. Differentiated individuals triangulate more than one offspring, diffusing the relative risk for psychological damage to children. Emotionally fused families show a more pronounced preference for triangulating a particular child, placing that offspring at serious risk for long-term damage to psychological functioning.

What Is the Objective of Therapy?

The primary objective is to help clients achieve a higher level of self-differentiation. A secondary objective is to translate intraindividual gains into more functional ways of responding to nuclear and extended family members.

What Produces Change?

At an individual level, change comes from motivated clients who achieve insight. They learn to distinguish and prefer cognitive rather than affective functioning. With improved cognitive functioning, individuals interact more functionally within their nuclear and extended families; essentially, intra-individual improvements generalize throughout the system. Change is hard won: "A lifetime of efforts to differentiate self may culminate in only slight changes in solid self" (Hall, 1983, p. 17). Gains benefit not just the current generation but future generations as well.

How Does Change Occur?

Improvements in self-differentiation occur once the marital dyad stabilizes; therapists achieve stability by regulating the amount of interaction between the dyad and focusing on cognitive over affective functioning. As anxiety decreases, listening improves and arguments lessen. Couples then work to develop a direct or person-to-person relationship with members of their respective family of origin. Through this reacquaintance process, relationships begin to reflect current reality rather than childhood experiences (e.g., adult offspring relate to their parents as individuals instead of roles). As personal relationships improve, the need for triangles diminishes.

How Does Treatment Proceed?

Therapy comprises two distinct phases:

- Nuclear family focus
  - ➢ Restricting sessions typically to the marital dyad to
    - ♦ emphasize that offspring are not to blame for any symptoms,
    - ♦ allow for using self to triangulate the couple.
  - ➢ Regulating anxiety within the session to
    - ♦ control the amount of direct interaction between the couple,
    - ♦ redirect discussions away from emotion toward cognition.
  - ➢ Using genograms to gather and assess historical information to
    - ♦ assess nodal events;
    - ♦ link historical processes to current functioning (e.g., replication of a pursuer–distancer pattern);
    - ♦ teach clients how to make similar linkages (e.g., identify each member's respective emotional "twin" from an earlier generation—the person who shared a comparable role within the family; examine "twin" for clues to current processes (Hall, 1983));
    - ♦ initiate phase two when clients demonstrate improvements in self-differentiation (i.e., a better relationship within the dyad).
- Extended family focus
  - ➢ Decreasing session frequency from weekly to monthly to
    - ♦ instill independence and responsibility in clients,
    - ♦ convey that familial relationship renegotiation is a life-long pursuit.

- ➢ Introducing Bowenian concepts.
- ➢ Encouraging members to explore their families of origin.
- ➢ Assigning the going-home task:
  - ♦ initiate some form of contact (e.g., telephone calls, letters, visits);
  - ♦ discourage confrontation or reconciliation;
  - ♦ encourage insight into client's role within the family's emotional system.
- ➢ Coaching clients on ways of achieving self-differentiation during subsequent contact:
  - ♦ form a direct relationship with individual family members,
  - ♦ keep conversations focused on those present,
  - ♦ share personal information.
- ➢ Terminating as extended family relations begin to improve.
- ➢ Offering booster sessions as needed.

What Is the Role of the Therapist?

Therapists coach or consult with clients on ways to enhance self-differentiation. They serve in a neutral role as observer or researcher of the family process, remaining calm and objective in-session. This behavior requires a high level of self-differentiation, which by definition means therapists are goal directed and autonomous, guided by personal principles rather than emotional responses. Thus, training typically includes identifying and resolving the therapist's own family-of-origin issues toward enhancing self-differentiation.

☐ Variants

Boszormenyi-Nagy

Contextual Family Therapy proposes that problems arise from premature efforts by parents to establish relational equity with offspring, typically through split filial loyalty (i.e., demands that the child side with one parent against another). These situations reflect the inheritance of unconscious and invisible loyalties, efforts by members to help their families at substantial cost to themselves (e.g., a child assuming a symptom to unite parents) (Boszormenyi-Nagy & Ulrich, 1981). Treatment consists of reestablishing fairness or relational equity among members by promoting the understanding of each other's perspective and the influence of historical context on functioning. Sessions typically involve the entire nuclear family, including the presence of children. Extended family may become involved through visits home to reexamine relational ties.

Framo

Family-of-Origin Therapy posits that problems reflect irrational role assignments such as the troublemaker (Framo, 1992). Treatment consists of a multicouples group format: clients discuss specific problems and group members offer insights. Framo's early work prepared couples to assemble siblings and parents for several family sessions aimed at reframing disturbing childhood memories as due to insufficient information. More recent work extends therapy beyond the dyad to include the entire family, toward determining how children and parents reciprocally maintain irrational role assignments or projective transference distortions (Framo, 1992).

PART

III

EXPERIENTIAL MODEL

9

CHAPTER

Experiential Family Therapy

Overview

The existential/humanistic psychology movement of the 1960s promoted emotional expression over psychoeducation or even insight as a critical means for enhancing individual growth. By extension, individual growth should improve communication across the family system, hence the emergence of a group of models known collectively as Experiential Family Therapy. This group is epitomized by the work of two highly charismatic individuals. Carl Whitaker, the originator of Symbolic-Experiential Family Therapy, used a provocative and sometimes outrageous style to decrease pretense so that a client would "become more of who he/she is" (Whitaker & Keith, 1981, p. 200). Virginia Satir, with her Human Validation Process Model (Satir & Baldwin, 1983), embraced an almost evangelical belief in the power of compassion and genuineness to heal all human problems. Additionally, several variants contribute important techniques to Experiential Family Therapy, most notably work by Walter Kempler, Fred and Bunny Duhl, and Leslie Greenberg and Susan Johnson. The chapter concludes with a summary of their technical contributions.

Basic Summary

Theory

- Repressed impulses and unexpressed emotion cause psychological dysfunction.

- Individual growth, freedom, and self-fulfillment improve family functioning.

Therapy

- The goal is to detect and express emotion.
- The therapist focuses primarily on changing individual functioning.

Therapist

- The therapist evokes overt expression of emotion.
- The therapist values spontaneity and genuineness in self and others.

Training

- Personal therapy is a critical prerequisite to practice.
- Therapy facilitates client and therapist growth.
- Supervision occurs through cotherapy with a more advanced therapist.

Origin and Evolution

Although trained in obstetrics and gynecology, Whitaker developed an unexpected interest in schizophrenia and switched to psychiatry. Severe personnel shortages of World War II limited his training to hospital administration and play therapy (Whitaker & Keith, 1981). After receiving a heavy clinical caseload at the Army's Oak Ridge Hospital in Tennessee, relative inexperience and stress lead him to experiment with and eventually prefer cotherapy as a standard treatment modality. Under this team format, the experiential aspect of his theory emerged. A series of spontaneous interventions, while novel, appeared to benefit clients (e.g., bottle feeding and rocking adult clients, wrestling confrontations between clients and therapists, awakening from having slept in-session to inform clients about his dreams). In 1946 he moved to Emery University's Department of Psychiatry and developed the symbolic aspect of therapy: the belief that all client utterances had covert meaning. While there, Whitaker organized several conferences on the treatment of schizophrenia, with attendees including Gregory Bateson and Don Jackson. When his unusual treatment strategies for schizophrenia came into question (i.e., aggressive play therapy to regress clients to an infantile state), Whitaker entered private practice with various colleagues from 1955 to 1965 (e.g., Thomas Malone, John Warkentin, Richard

Felder). He concluded his professional career at the University of Wisconsin Medical School and died in 1995. Followers include August Napier and David Keith.

As a trained social worker, Virginia Satir began private practice in 1951. In 1955, she created and taught the Family Dynamics Residency training program at the Illinois State Psychiatry Institute. Her work attracted the interest of Don Jackson, who requested that she join the early MRI group in 1959. While there, she developed and taught their family therapy training program. Satir left in 1966 to become Residential Program Director at the Esalen Institute in Big Sur, California, emerging as an important figure in the Human Potential Movement of the late 1960s and 1970s. Her background included a wide range of settings: psychiatric clinics, mental hospitals, residency treatment centers, public welfare programs, probation and parole services, and family service agencies (Satir, Stachowiak, & Tashman, 1975). Although Satir died in 1988, followers continue to promote her work through Avanta, The Virginia Satir's Network, an ongoing organization providing comprehensive training in this model.

☐ Key Terms

Whitaker viewed theory as a hindrance to clinical work—of concern only to novices until they found "the courage to give up theories and just live" (Whitaker, 1976, p. 154). Therapists should instead simply be themselves, a process isomorphic to client needs. Satir also deemphasized theory, believing it failed to capture the complexity of human experience. She acknowledged, however, that at a most basic level the individual struggles for growth, as measured by communication with other family members.

Terms from Whitaker

Black Sheep—the family member who functions worst or is considered crazy or ill; sacrifices self to provide the family with a common concern or focus (e.g., the problem behavior of a delinquent child).

White Knight—the family member who functions best or is considered "well"; sacrifices self to help the family achieve success (i.e., eventually self-destructs over the family's pressure to excel).

- The apparent mental health advantage of white knights over black sheep is illusory.
- Both are victims of the larger family system.

Battle for Structure—the initial phase of treatment characterized by the family's struggle to control therapy; it begins with the first phone contact when the therapist must dictate terms of therapy to ensure treatment success. Terms of therapy include appointment time and presence of a cotherapist, although typical battles center on who should attend sessions.

- The therapist should insist that all available members across three generations attend. This position
  - ➢ engenders treatment support by labeling extended family as "consultants,"
  - ➢ provides additional information to correct distorted views,
  - ➢ enhances spontaneity through the presence of children.
- If significant members failed to attend, Whitaker considered refusing to initiate treatment rather than working from a compromised position.

Battle for Initiative—follows the battle for structure; the therapist insists that family members assume responsibility for their own growth and life decisions. The family must

- determine the course of therapy (i.e., content),
- choose their own destiny (i.e., direction).

Terms from Satir

The Primary Family Triad—composed of the father, mother, and child; this is the foundation for how children learn about themselves and others. Determines

- coping mechanisms: "most stress patterns that individuals experience in their adult lives have their origin in the cradle" (Satir & Baldwin, 1983, p. 170);
- communication skills: incongruent messages (i.e., inconsistencies in affect and content) that damage the child's mental health and produce misinterpretations;
- self-esteem: exclusion from interaction between parents leads to a sense of rejection.

Metaphor—an image or association transposed across context to highlight similarities or differences (e.g., a child's play with doll represents treatment received from a parent). A central metaphor links self-esteem to the contents of a "pot":

- reflects Satir's farm background in which a cast iron pot served various purposes, from making soap or soup to storing manure (i.e., "a 3-S pot");

- quantifies self-esteem:
  - soap or soup is desirable or "high pot,"
  - fertilizer is undesirable or "low pot."

Communication Stance—one of five universal patterns of interaction that reflect various strategies for coping with emotion; all but the congruent stance are maladaptive because they suppress emotion, thereby producing physical symptoms.

- Placator—outwardly agreeable, inwardly disagreeable; sculpted as kneeling in supplication.
- Blamer—outwardly domineering, inwardly insecure; sculpted as standing with finger pointing accusingly.
- Computer (also known as a super-reasonable responder)—outwardly immobile, inwardly vulnerable; sculpted as standing rigidly with arms crossed.
- Distractor (also known as an irrelevant responder)—outwardly in constant motion, inwardly alienated; sculpted as limbs moving in different directions.
- Leveller (also known as congruent)—affect and behavior are consistent; sculpted as standing comfortably:
  - also valued in the therapist;
    - yields better diagnostic information through increased awareness (i.e., ability to separate personal issues from client problems),
    - ensures objectivity through centeredness (i.e., ability to maintain focus without concern for the past or future);
  - ways to foster:
    - recognize that "all feelings are honorable" (Satir, 1975a, p. 79),
    - detect the presence of emotion,
    - express when appropriate (e.g., the beginning of a first session is too soon to tell a client that he triggers sadness because of similarities with the therapist's recently deceased spouse (Satir & Baldwin, 1983)).

☐ Key Techniques

Whitaker was known for unusual interventions, such as sharing his erotic fantasies with families to show them that "sex is more open and fun if it involves all the generations" (Whitaker & Keith, 1981, p. 193). The purpose of these freewheeling, spontaneous, often irrational strategies was to enhance emotional expression by introducing "craziness" into families (i.e., creativity and zest). Satir believed that the therapist's own humanness or ability to personally connect with clients was more important than any specific technique (i.e., "My hands are my most valuable treatment asset" (Satir & Baldwin, 1983, p. 247)). While Whitaker relied on spontaneity to elicit underlying emotion, Satir used specific experiential exercises. Both agreed, however, that caring, genuineness, and personal involvement were critical factors determining successful therapeutic outcome.

Whitaker's Techniques (as outlined in Whitaker & Keith, 1981)

Redefining Symptoms as Attempts at Growth—depathologizing the problem by providing an absurd interpretation (e.g., asking a wife who reports that her husband has threatening her with violence, "How can you say he doesn't love you? Why else would he want to kill you?" (p. 211)).

Modeling Fantasy Alternatives to Actual Stressors—having clients consider imaginary alternatives to actual violence or inappropriate sexual behavior (e.g., asking a client who had previously attempted suicide, "If you were going to murder your husband, how would you do it?" or "Suppose when you got suicidal you decided you were going to kill me. How would you do it?" (p. 212)).

Separating Interpersonal from Intrapersonal Fantasy Stress—contaminating a client's fantasy by exploring how it might progress (e.g., asking a client with a previous suicide attempt to discuss what life would be like after her death, such as who her husband might remarry or how long her family would mourn).

Adding Pragmatic But Seemingly Inappropriate Bits of Intervention—once therapy is well underway, offering a number of interpretations that the family can accept or reject (e.g., remarking offhandedly to a husband whose wife is having headaches that spanking her might improve the symptoms).

Augmenting the Despair of a Client—heightening the anxiety of one member to generate family support (e.g., asking a schizophrenic son to evaluate the relative futility of attempting to stop parental arguments by accepting hospitalization).

Affective Confrontation—siding directly with one or more members against others (e.g., angrily telling parents who repeatedly attempt to intervene in a mock fight between the therapist and child to stop interrupting the process).

Treating Children Like Children and Not Peers—establishing a hierarchy so that adults supervise children (e.g., allowing children to tease or fight physically with the therapist but setting reasonable limits).

Satir's Techniques

Sculpting—a task in which the family graphically depicts the emotional system through gestures, postures, and spacing. Benefits of this task include

- providing more accurate information about family functioning than available through verbalization;
- revealing historical influences on current functioning because patterns likely replicate from each parent's primary triad (i.e., their father and mother and themselves as a child);
- releasing unexpressed emotion.

Family Stress Ballet—a task in which members assume the physical posture associated with various communication stances; the family spontaneously or at the therapist's directive begins shifting postures to experience the emotion associated with each new stance.

Ropes—a task for demonstrating system interrelations:

- direct family members to tie lengths of rope between each other,
- manipulate the ropes to demonstrate how current versus desired communication feels,
- augment with blindfolds to heighten the experience.

Family Reconstruction—a task for reexperiencing historical sources of influence; unrelated individuals serve as proxy family members.

- Gather a group of 10–20 individuals, including a designated Guide (i.e., therapist) and Star (i.e., main focus of the exercise).
- Develop Star's three-generational family history.
- Walk Star through the history as depicted by the other individuals present:
  - ➢ form a three-generational family map to indicate spatial relationships,
  - ➢ identify a circle of influence or individuals who played a formational role in Star's life,
  - ➢ reenact specific scenes so that Star becomes aware of outmoded coping strategies.

Parts Party—a task to facilitate awareness and acceptance of individual tendencies and unexpressed emotions (e.g., aggressiveness, fear).

- Gather a group of at least 10 individuals with a designated Guide and Host (i.e., person for whom the party is given).
- Direct Host to identify 6–10 Guests, preferably public figures who elicit attraction or repulsion.
- Assign a Guest role and descriptor to each individual present (e.g., John Wayne, strength).
- Use interaction of Guests to explore Host's internal conflicts (e.g., sexuality at odds with ambition and intelligence).
- Direct Guests toward cooperative resolution (e.g., aggression and intelligence unite to form effective leadership).

Basic Tenets

How Do Problems Arise?

Whitaker and Satir agreed on the source of problems, unexpressed emotion and denied impulses, although eliciting processes differed. For Whitaker, problems reflect inadequate attempts to handle tension and conflict from two sources:

- The actual marriage itself, which he envisioned as two scapegoats sent out by their respective families to perpetuate the original system (Whitaker & Keith, 1981). Those unable to integrate their backgrounds into a unified family experience manage associated conflict through avoidance of emotion and impulses.
- Situational stressors, such as transition to parenthood or job loss. Families unable to adapt to these changes avoid acknowledging emotion and impulses.

Satir traced problems to low self-esteem arising in the primary family triad. Parents who exclude children from interaction or use incongruent messages cause low self-esteem in offspring. Low self-esteem promotes the use of inadequate communication strategies. Blamers compensate for loneliness and failure by disagreeing indiscriminately. Placators compensate for rejection by being overly agreeable. Distracters compensate for alienation through denial. Computers compensate for vulnerability through intellectualizing.

How Do Problems Persist?

According to Whitaker, problems persist because families continue to suppress emotion and deny impulses, assuming that any other strategy would unleash uncontrollable and destructive conflict. Suppression diminishes the vitality needed to resolve the original problem (i.e., the marriage or situational stressor). Signs of diminished vitality include

- culturally invisible pathologies (i.e., behavior often dismissed as normal such as obesity, overwork, and heavy smoking);
- syndromes such as the "battle fatigued mother" or the "lonely father";
- destructive roles (e.g., white knight/black sheep).

Similarly, Satir believed that unexpressed emotion was energy that "does not go away just because feelings are not acknowledged ... [but would] resurface in destructive ways: physically, as an illness; intellectually, as in thought disturbances or limitations; or emotionally, as in nervousness or mental disorders" (Satir & Baldwin, 1983, p. 178).

What Is the Objective of Therapy?

According to Whitaker, the therapist and family work jointly to set specific goals; these goals often remain unconscious during therapy, identified only in retrospect. The therapy should

- improve emotional and behavioral congruence,
- enhance independence and free choice,
- expand the experiencing of emotion.

Satir believed that therapy should

- enhance individual expression of affect, behavior, and opinion among family members;
- recognize and incorporate individual uniqueness into decision making;
- encourage continued growth toward individual uniqueness.

What Produces Change?

Whitaker and Satir agreed that change requires a step backward or a temporary loss in functioning. Whitaker called the underlying change process regression and reintegration, or "falling apart and then reorganizing" (Whitaker & Keith, 1981, p. 192). Essentially, the family receives stress to the point of a transcendent experience—they come to view their situation from a completely different perspective. Emotions and impulses become unblocked. Outward manifestations of change are relatively small, "seen in the way the husband walks at the end of the interview ... [or] a change in voice tone" (p. 202).

Similarly, Satir believed that change follows a stage of chaos, as families become vulnerable to sensing and expressing potentially threatening feelings (i.e., "connected to their guts" (Satir, 1975b, p. 37)). They also learned to appreciate their own life force: the uniqueness and beauty inherent in every human being. Rather than abandoning their preferred dysfunctional communication stance, clients learn to "renovate" it (Satir & Baldwin, 1983). Placators transform submission into compassion. Blamers temper aggression with assertiveness. Computers use intelligence creatively rather than protectively. Distracters use irrelevance to introduce spontaneity and fun. As communication stances shift, emotions become overt and symptoms disappear.

How Does Change Occur?

Whitaker purposefully cultivated regression through exposing clients to anxiety inherent in provocative and evocative experiences (i.e., psychotherapy of the absurd). For example, he might suddenly disappear and later explain that he had to leave the session because his foot itched (Whitaker, 1975). Whitaker also increased anxiety through incongruent communication, such as saying with warmth, "Have you ever thought that killing yourself might make the family happy?" (Whitaker & Keith, 1981, p. 213). Thus, Whitaker would become crazier than the family, in a reversal of roles.

Satir purposefully cultivated chaos through exploring emergent emotion. In-session tasks also allow members to detect unexpressed emotion. Satir would then guide members toward finding appropriate ways to share this emotion within the family.

How Does Treatment Proceed?

Symbolic-Experiential Theory involves a three-stage process:

- Engagement
  - ➢ pursuing the battle for structure:
    - ♦ dictating terms of therapy (e.g., time and attendance),
    - ♦ rescheduling if multiple generations fail to attend, or complaining during the session about needing everyone present next time;
  - ➢ creating a therapeutic relationship:
    - ♦ demonstrating empathy through bilateral transference (e.g., adopting the family's language, accent, or rhythm of speech) and playing with children,
    - ♦ asking each member to describe the family and how it works,
    - ♦ assuming father is lonesome and question members about it,
    - ♦ assuming teaming (i.e., pairing off of members) and question members about it,
    - ♦ noting emotional distancing (i.e., suppression of affect) to target for later exploration;

- assessing the system, subsystems, and individuals:
  - taking a family history,
  - examining the family life cycle for clusters of key markers that cause stress (e.g., changes in income, family moves),
  - assessing each member's emotional age from clinical impressions (i.e., preoedipal innocence; conscientious, fact-oriented 5–8-year-old; presexual 7–9-year-old; homosocial 12–15-year-old; heterosocial 5–18-year-old),
  - assessing personal response for clues to functioning (e.g., anxiety, partial erection, depersonalized feelings);
- closing the session:
  - discouraging familial discussions between sessions to prevent bilateral pseudotherapy (i.e., misguided efforts to "straighten out" a family member),
  - issuing a double-bind if asked for feedback (e.g., telling the wife of an alcoholic that change seems unlikely given her hopeless dependence on her husband's drinking (Whitaker & Keith, 1981)).

- Involvement
  - beginning the battle for initiative:
    - becoming nondirective;
    - increasing anxiety and confusion through metaphor, teasing, humor, free association, fantasy, confrontation, or silence;
    - suspending any dialogue to work individually with the specific member displaying emotion;
    - getting that member to express emotion directly (e.g., consider comparisons with well-known fictional or public characters such as Archie Bunker or Richard Nixon to mentally represent intrapsychic problems and motivate change);
    - offering interpretations to increase anxiety and motivation (e.g., parents of a delinquent are asked if mother had a delinquent brother and father never had the courage to become delinquent as an adolescent (Whitaker & Keith, 1981));
    - noting any attempts to reject interpretations; such families fail to progress in therapy because they attempt to avoid anxiety.
- Disentanglement
  - observing family interaction;
  - refraining from intervening even if useful;
  - terminating quickly upon the family's request or if less stress is evident, including
    - signs of mutual enjoyment,
    - fewer sessions,
    - reduced interest in continuing (e.g., almost forgetting the session because of an outside interest);
  - considering individual therapy if requested.

Human Validation Process Model includes three stages:

- Stage one
  - ➢ validating each member through a personal connection:
    - ♦ initiating physical contact (e.g., shaking hands),
    - ♦ questioning that demonstrates interest,
    - ♦ showing a nonjudgmental attitude;
  - ➢ creating an informal atmosphere:
    - ♦ telling personal antidotes,
    - ♦ using humor;
  - ➢ assessing emotion, level of closeness:
    - ♦ asking questions about feelings,
    - ♦ avoiding an early focus on anger (i.e., an emotion for masking more vulnerable feelings) until the relationship develops further;
  - ➢ investigating the presenting problem:
    - ♦ sharing observations about implicit processes detected,
    - ♦ assessing through family sculpting, family stress ballet;
  - ➢ developing a working contract:
    - ♦ identifying mutual expectations,
    - ♦ specifying the length and number of sessions.
- Stage two
  - ➢ increasing confusion and disorder:
    - ♦ detecting emergent issues and pursue (e.g., the mother begins crying and her 10-year-old daughter crouches nearby; Satir asks the child about her reaction (Satir & Baldwin, 1983));
    - ♦ encouraging the expression of emotions (i.e., speaking the unspeakable);
    - ♦ probing for deeper emotion if anger surfaces;
    - ♦ clarifying faulty communication through questioning incomplete, distorted, or overly generalized statements;
    - ♦ offering interpretations that increase empathy.
- Integration (stage three)
  - ➢ recognizing the resolution of turmoil from the previous stage;
  - ➢ allowing for a period of emotional rest;
  - ➢ terminating therapy or reinitiate the cycle over a new issue.

What Is the Role of the Therapist?

The actual role of a Symbolic-Experiential therapist changes throughout therapy. Initially, the therapist is a "kindergarten teacher/shepherd" or a dominant parent of a young child (Whitaker & Keith, 1981, p. 209). The middle section involves being an age mate of the young child and then advisor to an older child. In the final section, the therapist is the retired parent of an adult child. Throughout, Whitaker advised working with a cotherapist to

- counteract the countertransference phenomena (i.e., compensate for one therapist becoming totally absorbed in the family's emotional field);
- enhance creativity and provide general support;
- offset the pathology of either therapist.

Whitaker believed that the therapist's personality and psychological functioning are key determinants of a successful outcome. He recommended acquiring an experiential background as part of training (e.g., individual therapy). This experience teaches the therapist to trust personal reactions as a valuable source of client information. Moreover, Whitaker encouraged therapists to use each session to enhance their own growth and achieve client goals. Given the nonrational aspect of this approach, prior research training is a potential hindrance to learning this model (Whitaker & Keith, 1981).

Satir believed that the therapist's role is to be firm yet caring, helping clients overcome their fear of sensing and expressing emotions. Similar to Whitaker, Satir promoted the use of personal responses to assess families. She warned that therapists must be aware of their own issues. They should work to become more congruent themselves, typically through personal growth exercises under the direction of a qualified trainer (e.g., re-create the trainee's primary triad with two proxy members, toward resolving residual problems of childhood). Growth is an ongoing process; thus, therapists should strive continually in- and out-of-session to maintain a "cutting edge" (Satir & Baldwin, 1983).

☐ Variants

Walter Kempler

Gestalt-Experiential Family Therapy views psychological problems as the result of incomplete encounters (i.e., interactions involving unexpressed feelings that then interfere with current perceptions and create uneasiness) (Kempler, 1981). Toward improving encounters, therapists activate enough emotion to create a "treatable crisis" or confrontation between family members. Techniques include

- using the "empty chair" scenario (i.e., clients pretend to interact with a missing family member, allowing them to identify and accept feelings and beliefs previously projected onto others);

- roleplaying scenes from childhood;
- establishing "ground rules" (e.g., no gossiping about missing persons, using statements instead of questions).

Fred and Bunny Duhl

Integrative Family Therapy comprises a blend of experiential, structural, behavioral, cognitive, and psychodrama. From this perspective, avoidance of shared feelings and perceptions leads to patterns of distance between family members. Techniques include

- spatializing (i.e., family sculpting) (Duhl, Kantor, & Duhl, 1973);
- puppetry (e.g., the therapist's use of a hand puppet to explore and validate a child's feelings of parental abandonment (Duhl & Duhl, 1981)).

Leslie Greenberg and Susan Johnson

Emotion-Focused Couples Therapy makes use of work from Fritz Perls, Satir, and MRI. From this approach, faulty attachment leads to suppression of "core" emotions and emergence of secondary reactive emotions (e.g., defensiveness, coercion). Therapists identify and validate the underlying emotion of both partners and work to change interactions based on this information. As outlined in Greenberg and Johnson (1988), techniques include

- empathetic reflection (i.e., identifying and accepting the underlying emotion such as "I can understand that you experience Harry's actions as rejecting and that it is painful to you" (p. 153));
- evocative responding (i.e., asking about personal responses such as "How do you feel?" or "What is it like for you?");
- experiments in awareness (i.e., expanding experience through repeating key sentences or using metaphors);
- framing difficulties as underlying vulnerabilities (e.g., "Is it ... hard for you to comfort her? ... Maybe you still want to stay behind that shield of yours we were talking about?" (p. 168)).

10

CHAPTER

Ethics

Understanding theory is only a part of what makes for a competent marriage and family therapist. Ethical dilemmas arise irrespective of theory and must be addressed. The primary governing body for MFT is the American Association for Marriage and Family Therapy (AAMFT). Thus, this chapter is based on a summary of their code of ethics, effective August 1, 1991. Because this is only a summary, and because updates occur periodically, a copy of the most recent AAMFT guidelines in their entirety should be obtained by anyone providing MFT services. Contact AAMFT, 1133 15th Street NW, Suite 300, Washington, DC 20005-2710, (202) 452-0109.

It is important to note that these guidelines apply to any member of AAMFT, regardless of membership category (e.g., Clinical Member, Approved Supervisor). Based on these guidelines, AAMFT pursues investigations of ethical violations; they also encourage reporting of unethical behaviors to appropriate professional associations and state regulatory boards. Moreover, investigations by AAMFT occur regardless of whether the member under question attempts to resign during the process. Any actions taken by the association (including resignation from AAMFT by the investigatee) are published for members to read. The Code of Ethics contains the following eight content areas.

1. As a Member of AAMFT, What Are Your Responsibilities to Clients?

- Do not discriminate or refuse to provide professional services based on the client's race, gender, religion, national origin, or sexual orientation.
- Do not exploit the trust and dependency of clients.
  - ➢ Avoid dual relationships with clients (e.g., business or close personal relationships) and take appropriate professional precautions when this is not possible.
  - ➢ Refrain from sexual intimacy with former clients for two years following termination of therapy.
  - ➢ Do not use the therapist–client relationship to forward any personal interests.
  - ➢ Respect a client's right to make decisions:
    - ♦ help in the evaluation of consequences;
    - ♦ advise clients that changes in marital status are their responsibility.
  - ➢ Continue therapy only when benefit to clients seems reasonably clear.
  - ➢ Assist individuals in obtaining other therapeutic services when unable/unwilling (for appropriate reasons) to provide care.
  - ➢ Avoid abandoning or neglecting clients without reasonable arrangements for treatment continuation.
  - ➢ Obtain written informed consent from the client before videotaping, audio recording, or third-party observation.

2. As a Member of AAMFT, What Are Your Responsibilities Involving Confidentiality?

- Do not disclose confidences:
  - ➢ unless mandated by law;
  - ➢ except to prevent a clear and immediate danger to the individual(s) at risk;
  - ➢ unless having obtained a written waiver from each legally competent individual member of the couple or family and only then according to conditions of the waiver; note without agreement from each legally competent member, the waiver cannot be used to disclose information received from any family member.
- Use any client-related materials for teaching, writing, or public presentation only after obtaining a written waiver as described above and only when appropriate steps to ensure the client(s) identity and confidentiality have been taken.
- Store and dispose of client records in ways that maintain confidentiality.

3. *As a Member of AAMFT, What Are Your Responsibilities for Professional Competence and Integrity?*

- Be aware of grounds for termination of AAMFT membership (and possibly other action):
  - ➢ a convicted felon;
  - ➢ convicted of a misdemeanor relating to qualifications or professional functions;
  - ➢ engaging in conduct that could lead to a conviction of the offenses as outlined above;
  - ➢ disciplined or expelled from a professional organization;
  - ➢ disciplined by a regulatory body (e.g., suspended licenses or certificates);
  - ➢ no longer competent to provide therapy (e.g., physical or mental impairment, abuse of alcohol or other substances);
  - ➢ uncooperative with AAMFT at any point during the entire process of investigating an ethical complaint.
- Seek appropriate professional assistance for personal problems that may impair clinical judgment or work performance.
- Be aware of teacher/supervisor responsibilities:
  - ➢ maintain high standards of scholarship,
  - ➢ present accurate information,
  - ➢ attempt to prevent distortion or misuse of clinical/research findings,
  - ➢ keep current of new knowledge through educational activities.
- Refrain from any harassment (e.g., sexual) or exploitation of anyone, including clients, students, trainees, supervisees, employees, colleagues, research subjects, and actual/potential witnesses to investigations or ethical proceedings.
- Refrain from diagnosing, treating, or advising on problems outside recognized areas of competence.
- Exercise caution when making public any professional recommendations or opinions.

4. *As a Member of AAMFT, What Are Your Responsibilities to Students, Employees, and Supervisees?*

- Avoid exploiting the trust/dependency of students, employees, and supervisees.
  - ➢ Make every effort to avoid dual relationships. If not possible, take precautions to ensure no exploitation or impairment to judgment result.
  - ➢ Do not provide therapy to students, employees, or supervisees.
  - ➢ Do not engage in sexual intimacy with students or supervisees.

- Do not allow students, employees, or supervisees to misrepresent their level of professional training, experience, or competence.
- Do not disclose supervisee confidences except
  - as mandated by law;
  - to prevent a clear and immediate danger to a person or persons;
  - when the therapist is a defendant in a civil, criminal, or disciplinary action arising from supervision, and only as directed as part of this action;
  - in training/educational settings involving multiple supervisors, and only then to other professional colleagues who are also responsible for the supervisee's training;
  - when a written waiver is obtained, and then only as directed by the waiver.

5. As a Member of AAMFT, What Are Your Responsibilities to Research Participants When You Conduct Research?

- Be aware of any federal and state laws/regulations or professional standards dictating standards of conducting research; observe safeguards to protect the rights of research participants.
- Seek ethical advice from qualified professionals not directly involved in the investigation if services to research participants may be compromised as part of research involvement.
- Inform participants about all aspects of their involvement that might reasonably influence the decision to participate. Be aware that participants may have potential impairments that limit their ability to communicate or understand the risks and benefits of participation.
- Allow participants to refuse or withdraw from the research study at any time; avoid dual relationships that would increase the risk of exploitation or impair professional judgment.
- Maintain confidentiality of information obtained from participants during the course of an investigation; when others (e.g., family members) might gain access, inform potential participants of the situation and any steps taken to protect confidentiality as part of informed consent.

6. As a Member of AAMFT, What Are Your Responsibilities to the Profession?

- Be accountable to the standards of the profession when serving as an employee or member of organizations.
- Use customary professional publication practices to assign publication credit to contributors based on relative contribution.
- When authoring books or other published materials,

  - ➢ give credit to the originator of any idea(s) used,
  - ➢ take reasonable precautions to ensure accurate portrayal of the facts in advertisements/promotions.
- Participate in improving the community/society (e.g., provide low cost services).
- Be committed to ensuring that MFT-related laws/regulations serve the public interest.
- Encourage public participation in provider regulation and service design/delivery.

7. As a Member of AAMFT, What Are Ethical Considerations Relating to Financial Arrangements?

- Follow accepted professional standards when making financial arrangements with clients, third-party payors, and supervisees.
  - ➢ Do not charge for referrals.
  - ➢ Do not charge excessive fees.
  - ➢ Disclose fee information at the beginning of services.
  - ➢ Represent information about services correctly.

8. As a Member of AAMFT, What Are Ethical Considerations Relating to Advertising?

- Represent MFT-related competence, education, training, and experience accurately.
  - ➢ Identify only those specialized areas that meet recognized professional standards.
  - ➢ Correct any inaccuracies made
    - ♦ by others about yourself,
    - ♦ by others about your employee(s).
- Do not misrepresent your responsibilities or aspects of practice.
- Do not use false, fraudulent, misleading, or deceptive professional identification.
- When publishing or advertising in any form of media, provide sufficient information so that the public can make an appropriate decision about professional services:
  - ➢ office information such as location and credit card acceptability,
  - ➢ appropriate degrees/state licensure or certification and AAMFT membership status,
  - ➢ description of your practice.
- When using the AAMFT designation
  - ➢ Place it in public information or advertisements upon receipt of designated title only.

  - Do not list status of application (e.g., pending Approved Supervisor).
  - Do not list AAMFT in the manner of an academic degree (i.e., initials after name).
  - Do not describe the AAMFT Approved Supervisor as an advanced clinical status.
  - As a student, associate, or affiliate, only list AAMFT status on a professional resume.
  - Do not imply organizational representation through the AAMFT name, logo, or abbreviated initials.
  - Use AAMFT membership only for clinical and professional activities.
  - As a clinical member, follow these guidelines when using the AAMFT name and related identifiers:
    - name, degree, license, or certificate held when required by state law;
    - business name (always after the member's name), address, and telephone number.
    - Do not include AAMFT offices held.
    - Do not list any specialization (i.e., it incorrectly implies credentialing through AAMFT).
- When listing educational qualifications
  - identify only degrees from regionally accredited institutions,
  - identify degrees from institutions recognized by states that license or certify marriage and family therapists (and only when AAMFT recognizes the state's regulation).
- Only AAMFT-accredited divisions and programs may use related designations in public information and advertising and only as specified in the Code of Ethics.
- Nonaccredited programs may not use AAMFT-related designators nor advertise that courses or training opportunities are accepted or meet membership requirements by AAMFT.

11

CHAPTER

Gender and Ethnicity

During the 1980s family therapists and theorists began discussing how factors such as ethnicity or gender influence the family system. Consequently, gender and ethnicity are now seen as critical underlying forces that influence the therapist and the family. In recognition of this influence, the Commission on Accreditation for Marriage and Family Therapy Education moved in 1988 to require that all accredited training programs address gender and ethnicity as separate classes or as imbedded across the entire curriculum. Thus, an overview of the field of MFT would be incomplete without at least some information on how these issues relate to therapy. In this chapter, each is considered briefly in turn. Essential and beneficial reading lists provide additional resources for further investigations into these important areas; see the References.

Gender

Family therapists have long acknowledged that gender comprises a fundamental organizing principle of human experience. Take, for example, Minuchin (1974) and Whitaker (1976) who each propose that families are ideally arranged hierarchically, so that parents are in charge of children. Fueled by the consciousness-raising groups of the 1960s, work by feminists in the late 1970s and early 1980s proposed that gender is yet another critical and often only implicitly recognized organizing principle influencing personal and social relationships.

Feminists view knowledge as largely socially constructed (i.e., reality is in the eye of the beholder), with commonly accepted views of gender as reflective of a patriarchally based culture that serves men's needs over that of women (McGoldrick, Anderson, & Walsh, 1989). This idea is captured in the phrase "the personal is political": patterns of unequal power distribution within the personal or family arena are isomorphic to the politics of the larger society.

Feminists criticize the field of MFT for its historical failure to attend to issues of gender. For example, the importance of changing performance within roles is emphasized, rather than challenging the roles themselves (e.g., Avis, 1985; Hare-Mustin, 1978). Mothers are often blamed for family difficulties because of traditional prescriptions that hold them primarily responsible for child-rearing. Additionally, therapists may be ill trained in recognizing and handling various forms of abuse and violence against wives and children. Abuse may be described in ways that obscure the agent of these acts, such as referring to wife battering as "spouse abuse" or "marital aggression" (Lamb, 1991). More recently, there is acknowledgment that the same culturally prescribed roles that diminish women's power within the family also constrain men. Avis (1996) concludes that even relative privilege is not without cost. Fathers, for example, are often given a more peripheral role in their children's lives, particularly after a divorce.

What has emerged from this work is not a single entity called "feminist family therapy" but instead a general perspective that promotes awareness of gender and power relations across theories (i.e., gender sensitivity). If gender is a socially constructed idea that maintains the status quo of inequality, it follows that a goal of feminist-informed therapy is to deconstruct such views. There is no formula or set of techniques for handling what is viewed as a pervasive problem at a cultural level (McGoldrick et al., 1989). Instead, therapists adopt a collaborative style aimed at facilitating equality among men and women and are supportive of clients' rights to live their lives outside of culturally prescribed roles. Thus, therapists can use this perspective to enrich their work with any particular model of MFT.

Ethnicity

Concern with oppression, or the forceful subordination of a specific group of individuals, arises also as a primary theme relating to issues of ethnicity. Here too the field of MFT has been criticized for another form of bias, that of ethnocentricity. The American middle-class Anglo ideal has been used as the yardstick for determining "normalcy," without recognition that families from dissimilar cultures, social classes, or structural compositions may have differing values.

Fontes and Thomas (1996) provide a useful classification system for work in this area—either as culture specific or multicultural. The former comprise a growing body of literature relating to how therapists should proceed with various groupings of individuals. Such guides provide information on how cultural influences might affect various aspects of family functioning, including expression of affect or parenting practices. They describe, however, the average person within a respective group and may promote the "myth of sameness" or a deemphasis of the vast individual differences inherent in any group (Hardy, 1989). Differences in acculturation (i.e., accommodation to the dominant culture), for example, may yield vastly different customs within a group of emigrants from the same native country.

In contrast, multicultural works promote an investigative approach to any family, with the therapist becoming an anthropologist of sorts in allowing members to define their own unique culture (e.g., Schwartzmann, 1983). Here the emphasis is often on promoting self-discovery of personal values, positions, and assumptions toward understanding how these factors influence assumptions about therapy. A reading of both specific and multicultural works offers perhaps the best strategy for learning of commonalties across particular cultures, while maintaining an appreciation for individual differences in each group.

Consistent with the view espoused by feminists, a culturally sensitive therapist recognizes that therapy is not a value-free endeavor. Awareness is the first step toward avoiding problems such as tendencies to pathologize that which is different. From this perspective, the therapist need not share the same culture as the client but instead should be open to learning about each client's unique cultural background. Culturally sensitive therapists also seek to validate strengths derived from various backgrounds as one way to empower clients toward gaining greater mastery over their lives.

12

CHAPTER

Model Comparisons

Models of family therapy seem to merge together when they are learned initially. Differences between a few of the models are clear, but between others, the differences may seem more artificial than real. Only after repeated exposure to their various elements, assumptions, and treatment formats do model distinctions become clear. This chapter recapitulates the major features of the models. In each section some of the words are italicized; we think these are key words that may help you recall important elements within the model.

Dimension	Model	
	Strategic	**Communication (MRI)**
Key Figures	Haley, Madanes	Bateson, Erickson, Fisch, Fry, Jackson, Watzlawick, Weakland
Key Terms	*Power*—who in the system is in the position to make decisions about rules; *Triangle*—assumes that problems occur when a power struggle between two people forces the involvement of a third person.	*Reality*—perception based and depends on how and where the perceiver instills order; *Communication*—the act of sending or receiving information; *Relationship*—not an entity but an interaction with meanings assigned to the ongoing behaviors; *Equifinality*—different beginnings may produce similar outcomes; *Equipotentiality*—similar beginnings (i.e., events) may produce dissimilar effects; *Pars-pro-toto*—parts can substitute for the whole; *Change*—first and second order.
Key Techniques	*Ordeals*—therapist attaches an aversive, yet constructive, activity to the presenting problem; *Paradoxical Directives*—prescribing the symptom, restraining change, positioning; *Reframing; Positive Connotation; Symptom Manipulation.*	*Reframing*—changing conceptual or emotional viewpoint to allow client to experience the situation differently yet fit the "facts" of the situation; *Utilizing resistance*—therapist asks that client slow down or not change; *Symptom Manipulation*—therapist alters when, how, and where a symptom appears.
How do problems arise?	A symptom occurs when there is a *power struggle* in the system, because of either an *inadequate hierarchy* or *conflict* between two individuals; symptoms reflect specific behavioral interactions in the family.	A problem, and the distress it produces, occurs when a smaller problem is *mishandled,* and the mishandling produces more *distress.*
How do problems persist?	*Rigid behavioral sequences* maintain the problem, and once established, symptoms associated with the problem act as *homeostatic mechanisms* regulating family interaction patterns.	Once occurring, attempted *solutions* to remedy the problem usually *vary only slightly,* in effect, doing more of the same. This makes the problem worse. Once established, *interactional patterns* among relevant individuals maintain the problem.
Therapy Objective	Removing the *presenting problem.*	The goal is to *reduce distress* by removing or reducing the problem by either *changing interactions* (i.e., making the problem nonexistent) or *perceptions* (i.e., viewing the problem as less distressing).
What produces change?	Change occurs when the family engages in *new behavioral sequences* that are *incompatible* with the ones associated with the presenting problem.	Change occurs when *altering* either *perception* or *behavior* reduces *distress.*

(*continued*)

Dimension	Model	
	Strategic	**Communication (MRI)**
How does change occur?	Shifts in relevant *interaction sequences* occur in small *increments*; each incremental modification reflects the amount of behavior change mandated by the assigned *out-of-session* task.	Changes *interactions* associated with the problem, specifically altering those *behavioral* and *perceptual* patterns that have accompanied previous attempts to fix the problem. Intervention involves at least two people.
Therapist Role	Is *active, directive,* and *assumes responsibility* for implementing change. This change occurs through tasks, either direct or paradoxical.	Therapist is *responsible* for changing the client's *response* to the distressing situation. Does this by seeking compliance to *task assignments* and by shifting the client's *frame of reference* about the problem and subtly encouraging new ways of attacking the problem.

Dimension	Model	
	Solution Focused	**Narrative**
Key Figures	Berg, deShazer, O'Hanlon, Weiner-Davis	Epston, White
Key Terms	Exceptions	*Unique outcomes*—occasions when the problem did not occur although the likelihood was high that it should have occurred.
Key Techniques	*Exceptions*—when the problem did not occur or was not as bad; *Miracle Question*—hypothetical scenario that allows the client and therapist to assess what perceived differences need to occur to lessen the problem and, consequently, the goal of therapy; *Scaling*—quantifying the needed, desired, or current levels of behavior.	*Questions*—the therapist directs the family to address how the problem has affected their lives, and vice versa; *Externalization and Stories*—Families are encouraged to reconstruct the problem as an outside entity, to observe and label its attributes, and then fight against its character.
How do problems arise?	Model does not address	Model does not address
How do problems persist?	The presence of an ongoing problem creates a *narrowing of perspective,* limiting perceived alternative behaviors that would allow change.	The family becomes *problem saturated*—unable to attend to or view the world beyond their relationship to the problem.
Therapy Objective	To *think* differently about problem, to *talk* differently about the problem, or to *do something different* with the problem.	To *instill a sense* in the family that the problem is not within an individual, but outside of family, and is *controllable*.
What produces change?	Acknowledging that the problem is not always *present, overbearing,* or *beyond control.*	A *change* in *perspective* by the family about its ability to handle and *fight the problem*.

(*continued*)

Dimension	Model	
	Solution Focused	**Narrative**
How does change occur?	*Finding* and *reacting* to *exceptions* to the perception of problem omnipotence.	*Directed stories* (along with letters and certificates) allow the family to *reconceptualize* the problem as no longer oppressive.
Therapist Role	Use the client's *existing resources, remove impediments* to change, and help the client develop ways of *allowing* the desired behavior to occur.	The therapist provides the *questions* and new *frame of reference* that the family uses to reconceptualize the problem's assumed omnipotence.

Dimension	Model	
	Milan (Systemic)	**Psychoeducational**
Key Figures	Boscolo, Cecchin, Gianfranco, Hoffman, Penn, Prata, Selvini-Palazzoli, Tomm	Anderson, Falloon, Goldstein
Key Terms	*Invariant prescription*—all families receive the same task; *Family rules, games, and myths*—mechanisms used by the family to maintain interactions patterns that perpetuate the problem.	*Expressed emotion*—the level of critical, hostile, or intrusive comments made by family members about the absent patient during a structured interview; *Diathesis-stress* model—environmental factors influence illness onset and progress among individuals with a genetic predisposition for specific diseases (e.g., schizophrenia); *Benign indifference*—a neutral style of interaction purposefully encouraged in family members.
Key Techniques	*Positive connotation*—reframes the symptom so that it appears to serve a positive function within the family; *Therapeutic ritual*—is framed as an experiment, prescribing a time and place for the behavior to occur; it is sometimes used to exaggerate family rules or myths, or used to accentuate the positive connotation that has been constructed to explain the symptom; *Circular questions*—a method of gathering information while forcing the examination of processes internal to the system.	One day workshop to *dispense information* about the illness; use of techniques from Structural and Behavioral Family Therapy models.

(*continued*)

Dimension	Model	
	Milan (Systemic)	**Psychoeducational**
How do problems arise?	Rules governing the system are *too rigid*.	*Environmental factors affect onset* among those individuals with a *genetic predisposition* toward the disorder. Accordingly, symptoms are products of the disease, and although influenced by environmental factors, they serve *no function* within the family system.
How do problems persist?	The symptom or sick person becomes the *stabilizing agent* for the system, and the system, in turn, *organizes itself* around the problem.	*Highly negative* or *excessively intrusive* environments are difficult for the patient to tolerate, consequently producing physiological arousal and symptom exacerbation.
Therapy Objective	*Introduce information* into the system to alter family rules, games, or myths; *no specific* behavioral goals are negotiated with the family.	Therapy seeks to *postpone relapse*. *Postponement* is a critical goal; with every relapse, patients typically experience increasingly severe decrements in functioning.
What produces change?	Treatment seeks to *induce flexibility* into the system and *broaden* the range of acceptable behaviors; change occurs randomly as *information* is added to the system.	Family environments that are *less negative* (lower expressed emotion) and *better organized* around the illness.
How does change occur?	Symptom alleviation follows *interaction changes* brought about by therapeutic *rituals* or *prescriptions*, and *in-session questions*.	*Education* about the illness, encouragement of *nonfamilial social contact*, and *therapy* that encourages reasonable limit setting and reshaping *appropriate individual and intergenerational boundaries*.
Therapist Role	Attempts to maintain a *neutral stance* with the family while acting as a *conduit* to the other therapy team members.	Therapist is *active* and *directive* and serves as a *liaison* between the medical treatment team and the family.

Dimension	Model	
	Behavioral	**Cognitive Behavioral with Couples and Families**
Key Figures	Alexander, Liberman, Patterson, Reid, Stuart, Webster-Stratton	Jacobson, Beck, Margolin, Weiss, Epstein, Baucom
Key Terms	*Coercive interactions*—process of parent request → aversive child response → parent acquiesce; child is reinforced for noncompliance; *Reciprocity*—the equitable exchange of positives or negatives among family members.	

(*continued*)

Dimension	Model	
	Behavioral	Cognitive Behavioral with Couples and Families
Key Techniques	*Parents skills training; Contingency contracting*—a contract outlining desired and undesired behaviors.	Uses questioning and logic to expose faulty cognitive patterns and beliefs. Uses standard behavioral change techniques.
How do problems arise?	*Parents are trainers* for inappropriate aggressive and antisocial behavior. *Beginning in the home*, and occurring before adolescence, it starts with confrontations between parent and child during discipline. Some children have a *constitutional predisposition* (i.e., temperament) for antisocial or aggressive behavior.	Faulty beliefs and cognitions brought into the relationship or that evolve in the relationship influence behavior.
How do problems persist?	Once established, *inadequate skills* and *inappropriate reinforcement* maintain most problems. These at-risk children are *rejected* by peers at school and are raised in a home characterized by high levels of negativity.	Behavioral patterns reflect *faulty cognitions* and, once established, are difficult to change.
Therapy Objective	*Teach* parenting skills and remove or alter impediments to *effective parenting* sufficient to alleviate the presenting problem.	Change the *problem behavior* along with the *cognitions* associated with the behavior.
What produces change?	Change occurs when the parents *alter environment contingencies* that control the behavior.	Correct *faulty cognitions* and reinforce *positive couple interaction*.
How does change occur?	Altering the environmental contingencies tied to the problem. The problem reduces to three behavioral features: antecedents, behaviors (problem), and consequences (ABCs). Parents are taught how to *modify* their *own behavior*, their *environment*, and the *child's behavior*.	Examine the *fallacy* of the cognitions and *create* or *reinforce* new situations that change the couple's *interaction*.
Therapist Role	Is a *teacher* of skills and consultant to the parents. *Takes responsibility* for getting the parents to implement the new skills.	*Teaches* the couple or family how to examine beliefs, cognitions, and how to subsequently *engage* in new behaviors.

Dimension	Model	
	Experiential	Structural
Key Figures	Duhl & Duhl, Kempler, Satir, Warkentin, Whitaker	Aponte, Fishman, Minuchin, Montalvo

(*continued*)

Dimension	Model	
	Experiential	**Structural**
Key Terms	*Whitaker: Battle for structure*–the initial phase of treatment characterized by the family's struggle to control therapy; *Battle for initiative*–follows the battle for structure; the therapist insists that family members assume responsibility for their own growth and life decisions. *Satir: Primary family triad*–the foundation for how children learn about themselves and others; *Communication stance*–universal patterns of interaction that reflect various strategies for coping with emotion.	*Structure*–behavior patterns organized to fulfill the functions of the family; *Boundaries* (diffuse, clear, rigid); *Coalition*–two family members regularly join against a third.
Key Techniques	*Whitaker* (selected)–Redefining symptoms as attempts at growth; Modeling fantasy alternatives to actual stressors; Augmenting the despair of a client. *Satir: Sculpting*–family graphically depicts the emotional system through gestures, postures, and spacing; *Ropes*–demonstrating system interrelations; *Family reconstruction*–reexperiencing historical sources of influence; *Parts party*–facilitate awareness and acceptance of individual tendencies and unexpressed emotions.	*Enactment*–forcing the family to engage in behavioral patterns associated with the presenting problem; *Raising intensity*–therapist manipulates affect intensity to destabilize patterned transactions within the family; *Joining*–through accommodation, tracking, and mimesis.
How do problems arise?	*Unexpressed* emotion and *denied* impulses.	*Inadequate family structure* occurs where needed; rule and structure changes do not occur (e.g., developmental stage) or parental conflict is present.
How do problems persist?	*Whitaker:* Families continue to *suppress emotion* and *deny impulses*, assuming that any other strategy would unleash uncontrollable and destructive conflict; suppression diminishes the vitality needed to resolve the original problem. *Satir* held a similar position.	Continued problem behavior represents the *fulfillment* of actions consistent with the *faulty structure*.
Therapy Objective	Improve *emotional* and *behavioral congruence*, enhance independence and free choice; expand the experiencing of *emotion* and *continued growth*; recognize and incorporate *individual uniqueness* into decision making.	*Change* the *structure* and remove the symptom.

(*continued*)

Dimension	Model	
	Experiential	**Structural**
What produces change?	Change requires a step backward or a temporary *loss in functioning* followed by a process of regression and *reintegration*, or "falling apart and then *reorganizing*" or *renovating* previous dysfunctional communication patterns.	New *transactional* patterns are introduced that reinforce *appropriate hierarchies* and *strengthen boundaries*.
How does change occur?	*Whitaker:* cultivated *regression* by exposing clients to *anxiety* inherent in *provocative* and *evocative* experiences (i.e., psychotherapy of the absurd). *Satir:* cultivated chaos by exploring *emergent emotion* using tasks that allowed members to detect *unexpressed* emotion.	Therapist uses *in-session* techniques to alter family interaction; also challenges and attempts to modify *attributional sets* and beliefs that inhibit the needed structural changes.
Therapist Role	Use each session to *enhance personal* (therapist) growth and *facilitate* client growth; enhance client creativity and provide general support; teach clients to overcome their fear of *sensing* and *expressing* emotions. *Trust* emotional reactions and model this behavior for clients.	Forces interaction pattern changes by giving *advice, raising intensity*, using humor, altering *transactions*, and challenging *attributional sets*.

Dimension	Model	
	Object Relations	**Bowenian**
Key Figures	Ackerman, Boszormenyi-Nagy, Framo, Scharff & Scharff, Schnarch, Siegel, Skynner	Bowen, Fogarty, Friedman, Kerr
Key Terms	*Differentiation of self*—emotional detachment or the ability to maintain objectivity by separating affect from cognition; *Emotional fusion*—the inability to separate emotions from cognition; *Emotional cutoff*—extreme forms of distancing between members in emotionally fused families; *Nuclear family emotional process*—relationship strategies used by spouses to handle anxiety; *Family projection process*—spiraling levels of emotional illness transmit across successive generations through the child dysfunction strategy.	*Genograms*—a diagram of the family's genealogy typically depicting three generations; *Going home task*—clients establish contact with their family of origin; *I-position*—requests or statements that emphasize the speaker's personal responsibility for attitudes, behavior, or affect.

(*continued*)

Dimension	Model	
	Object Relations	**Bowenian**
Key Techniques	*Empathic listening*—concerted attention to detect the latent meaning behind speech or interactions; *Interpretation*—offering the subjective meaning or motive behind behavior, affect, or opinions; *Countertransference*—analysis of spontaneous reactions toward a client's transference phenomena, a vital source of information about intrapsychic deficits.	*Genograms*—a diagram of the family's genealogy typically depicting three generations; *Going home task*—clients establish contact with their family of origin; *I-position*—requests or statements that emphasize the speaker's personal responsibility for attitudes, behavior, or affect.
How do problems arise?	Reflect *intrapsychic deficits* in one or more family members originating in *early childhood trauma* and typically involve inadequate parenting.	Individuals display symptoms during *situational* or *chronic stress; emotionally fused* individuals experience more symptoms (than differentiated counterparts) largely because they have *fewer strategies* for handling stressors (e.g., less adaptive coping skills).
How do problems persist?	Problems persist because families are involved in a process of *unconscious collusion* in perpetuating the *projective identification process.*	*Family projection processes* (i.e., emotional distance, marital conflict, spousal dysfunction, and child dysfunction) engaged in by *emotionally fused individuals* continuously produce problems.
Therapy Objective	Client must *release* and *accept repressed* or *forgotten* material, thus allowing family members to react to each other based on current reality rather than images of the past.	Achieve a higher level of *self-differentiation.*
What produces change?	Achievement of whole object relations occurs with the *integration* of *good and bad* objects.	Clients who achieve *insight* learn to distinguish and *prefer cognitive* rather than affective functioning.
How does change occur?	Individuals must process *insight:* information should produce an outward and desirable manifestation in the client's life. May require clients to *relive* and *mourn* unfulfilling aspects of past relationships, thereby garnering significant relief from *insufficient parenting* received during childhood.	Through reacquaintance processes (*family of origin work*), relationships begin to reflect *current reality* rather than childhood experiences (e.g., adult offspring relate to their parents as individuals instead of roles). As personal relationships improve, *family projection processes* diminish.
Therapist Role	Assume a *nondirective* stance; offer *interpretations* designed to generate new discussions by revealing *hidden motivations* or *avoided emotions.*	*Coach* clients on ways to enhance self-differentiation and serve in a neutral role as *observer* or researcher of the family process, remaining *calm* and *objective* in-session.

13 CHAPTER

Questions

We include this chapter to help you prepare for an examination in family therapy. The format of the questions varies. Each variation slightly changes the method used to recall the material. Some answers are obvious; some require that you reread the section associated with the material. Answers to the multiple choice and matching are given at the end of the chapter.

Multiple Choice

1. Which is not true of schizophrenia:
   (a) Disturbed family communication (e.g., the double-bind) causes this illness.
   (b) Patients fare better in families displaying lower levels of expressed emotion.
   (c) Psychoeducational approaches garner improved outcomes.
   (d) Insight-based models are detrimental to recently released patients.

2. A "3-S" pot is a metaphor associated with which model:
   (a) Strategic
   (b) Ordeal
   (c) Object Relations
   (d) Satir

3. Tim (63) and his wife Donna (49) have been attending therapy with their daughter Briana (29). Since her divorce, Briana and her daughter

Tiffany (9) have been living with Tim and Donna; therapy has addressed Tiffany's adjustment in the new household. Because Tiffany is close to her father, Briana believes that the session information should be of interest to him. She calls the therapist and requests that a copy of the weekly progress notes be sent to Tiffany's father. To do so, the therapist must get a written release from
(a) Briana
(b) Tiffany's father
(c) Tim, Donna, and Briana
(d) Tim, Donna, Briana, and Tiffany's father

4. Which models view unexpressed emotion as problematic to functioning:
(a) Bowen Systems
(b) Symbolic-Experiential
(c) Psychoeducational
(d) Ordeal

5. What is not recommended for schizophrenics and their family members?
(a) encouraging an attitude of benign indifference
(b) providing the family with information about how the illness arises
(c) allowing family members to vent frustration in the presence of the patient
(d) Structural Family Therapy

6. Which model does not support the idea that therapists should undergo therapy as part of their professional training and development?
(a) Bowen Systems
(b) Object Relations
(c) Human Validation Process
(d) MRI

7. Out of earshot of Dad, Mom points out one of his parenting inadequacies to the children. From a Contextual Family Therapy perspective, Mom's actions are evidence for
(a) split filial loyalty
(b) diffuse boundaries
(c) entitlement
(d) triangulation

8. Bill (50) and Alexandria (43) present for therapy because their son Ralph (13) has developed a school phobia. The phobia emerged after a trial separation between Bill and Alexandria. Bill moved back into the home when it became apparent that the only way to get Ralph

to attend school was with both parents working together to help him. From Boszormenyi-Nagy's perspective, this is an example of
(a) invisible loyalties
(b) emotional divorce
(c) fusion
(d) enmeshment

9. From Behavioral Family Therapy's perspective, the scenario given in question 8 is an example of
(a) positive reinforcement
(b) extinction
(c) coercion
(d) shaping

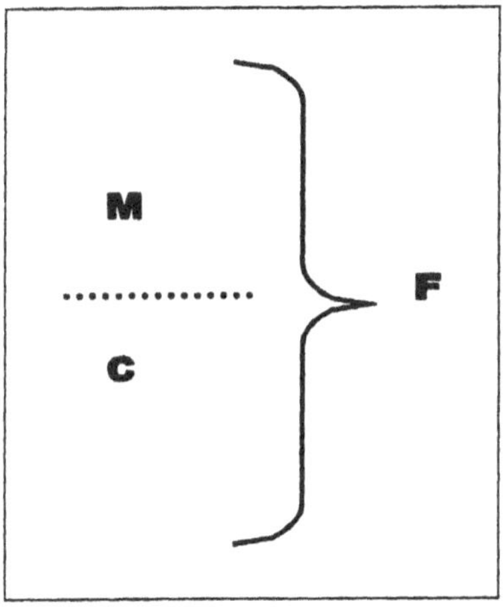

10. This diagram is from which model?
(a) Bowen Systems
(b) Structural
(c) Ordeal
(d) Object Relations

11. Bob (45) and Marianne (38) argue about what is the proper age for their daughter Jill (14) to begin dating. Jill hears the fighting and enters the room. Marianne draws Jill into the argument to side with her against Bob. From a Bowen Systems perspective, what has occurred?
(a) triangulation
(b) diffusion
(c) split filial loyalty
(d) battle for structure

12. From a Structural perspective, what has occurred in the above scenario?
(a) triangulation
(b) coalition
(c) enmeshment
(d) enactment

13. Which theory believes that relative birth order is significant in determining specific characteristics?
    (a) Structural
    (b) Bowen Systems
    (c) Experiential
    (d) MRI

14. Creation of a sufficient holding environment is a critical part of which theoretical approach?
    (a) MRI
    (b) Bowen
    (c) Object Relations
    (d) Experiential

15. Sally (32) and Nathan (41) seek help with how to handle their 5-year-old son, Timothy. Timothy's aggression in school dates back to a biting incident in preschool. Sally and Nathan report a relatively trouble-free marriage with almost no conflict, not at all like their respective parents who fought continually before divorcing. The therapist notices that they are especially cautious about not wanting to contradict one another. Several sessions later, a discussion between Sally and Nathan gives way to a sizable quarrel, complete with yelling and cursing. A Structural Family therapist would interpret the fight as evidence of
    (a) marital discord
    (b) inadequate boundaries
    (c) rigidity
    (d) negative reinforcement

16. Jonathan (47) and Samantha (46) present for help with their daughter Michelle (12) who has had a history of depression. The family has also recently moved and Michelle will be entering a new high school this fall. The family spends some time animatedly describing recent events in their lives that they believe deepened Michelle's depression. The conversation begins to wind down. An Object Relations therapist would be most likely to
    (a) assure the parents that many 14-year-olds feel down sometimes
    (b) present basic information on depression
    (c) request details of their earlier histories
    (d) ask the family to enact the morning of Michelle's first day at school

17. From an Object Relation's view, a client's use of unusual phrasing is potential evidence for
    (a) diffuse boundaries
    (b) collusion
    (c) irrational role assignment
    (d) a derivative

18. During a recent session, Anthony (41) tells the therapist of his increasing frustration and anger with a former girlfriend who is now dating a former best friend. Anthony states that if she does not break off the relationship, he will kill her. He has even thought of a detailed plan to do so. The therapist should
    (a) tell the police
    (b) tell the former girlfriend and former best friend
    (c) wait until the next session scheduled in two weeks to see if Anthony is still angry
    (d) tell the police and the former girlfriend

19. Diffuse boundaries are described in which theory(ies)
    (a) Structural only
    (b) Structural and MRI
    (c) Structural and Object Relations
    (d) Structural and Experiential

20. Introjects can only be detected by
    (a) external observers
    (b) other family members
    (c) trained therapists
    (d) the symptom bearer

21. The tendency of a system to regulate itself in order to maintain a constant internal environment in response to changes in the external environment:
    (a) equifinality
    (b) homeostasis
    (c) equipotentiality
    (d) morphorgenesis

22. During their first marital therapy session, Frank (24) and Linda (19) describe themselves as extremely unhappy with their five-month marriage. They also report a number of episodes involving domestic violence. Linda begins to cry and asks the therapist for advice on whether their marriage is worth saving. The therapist should
    (a) advise them to attempt a trial separation
    (b) give them the name of a good divorce lawyer
    (c) advise them that a divorce is their decision
    (d) recommend a divorce given the domestic violence

23. The following theorist is most associated with power and control:
    (a) Haley
    (b) Minuchin
    (c) Freud
    (d) Bateson

24. Which of the following model(s) use metaphor?
    (a) MRI
    (b) Human Validation Process
    (c) Strategic
    (d) All of the above

25. The following therapist is most associated with boundaries and hierarchies:
    (a) Haley
    (b) Minuchin
    (c) Bowen
    (d) Bateson

26. The following therapist is most associated with multigenerational processes of psychopathology:
    (a) Haley
    (b) Minuchin
    (c) Bowen
    (d) White

27. The Milan approach is characterized by the following techniques:
    (a) circular questioning
    (b) invariant prescription
    (c) family triangle
    (d) A & B
    (e) A & C

28. In Psychoeducational Family Therapy, after the hospital release and initial intervention (i.e., day-long workshop), which of the following occurs next to reduce relapse in families with a schizophrenic member?
    (a) Strategic
    (b) MRI
    (c) Solution Focused
    (d) Structural and Behavioral
    (e) Externalization and MRI

29. At the close of a session, Ann (45), a stockbroker of 10 years, mentions a "hot" stock tip to her therapist. The therapist should
    (a) use part of the next session to discuss the tip in more detail
    (b) call a different stockbroker to place an order for the stock
    (c) refrain from pursuing the stock purchase
    (d) pass the tip along to a colleague

30. AAMFT states that therapists must refrain from sexual involvement with clients:

(a) only during the actual course of therapy
(b) until two months have passed since termination
(c) no matter how much time has passed since termination
(d) for two years after termination

31. Which model will sometimes use ordeals to alter symptom expression?
(a) Strategic
(b) MRI
(c) Solution Focused
(d) Structural
(e) Externalization

32. Most strategic tasks have a common characteristic—they try to manipulate:
(a) the entire family
(b) only the person with the symptom
(c) the symptom
(d) only two people, one of which is the symptom carrier
(e) the person least invested in changing

33. Which two models are concerned about family hierarchy and its influence on symptom development?
(a) Strategic/Structural
(b) MRI/Strategic
(c) Solution Focused/MRI
(d) Structural/MRI
(e) Externalization/Structural

34. According to MRI (i.e., Bateson), all communication contains which of the following two levels or functions?
(a) digital and analog
(b) report and command
(c) verbal and nonverbal
(d) receiver and sender

35. Behavioral Family Therapy has recently increased the importance of
(a) feeling statements
(b) anger control skills
(c) cognitions and attributions
(d) contingency contracting

36. Treatment for almost all forms of sexual dysfunction typically involves
(a) dilators
(b) squeeze technique
(c) desensitization
(d) medication

37. An MRI-based therapist working with a client with stage fright is most likely to tell the client:
    (a) to try harder to relax when on stage
    (b) to increase daily time devoted to practice
    (c) to identify the disadvantages of improvement
    (d) to explore early memories associated with the fear

38. The squeeze technique describes
    (a) Minuchin's view of how family members become peripheral
    (b) A sex therapy technique used in the treatment of premature ejaculation
    (c) LoPiccolo's self-stimulation paradigm
    (d) Method used in conjunction with sensate focus to treatment vaginismus

39. The influence of feminism on the field of MFT has yielded all but
    (a) a set of specific techniques for challenging the status quo
    (b) a general perspective for increasing awareness of cultural biases
    (c) an appreciation for how even privilege produces costs
    (d) awareness that the personal is political

40. In working with an anorexic client, a Structural therapist would be most likely to
    (a) ask the family to attend a lunchtime session to observe patterns around eating
    (b) ask the family to change chairs so that everyone experiences the deficient holding environment
    (c) ask the family to show up with the grandparents in an effort to increase spontaneity
    (d) ask the anorexic to identify those parts of herself that are associated with the early trauma

☐ Matching

Associate the Concept with the Therapy Model

Strategic	( )	A. growth
Structural	( )	B. failed solutions
MRI	( )	C. differentiation/I-position
Milan	( )	D. unresolved conflicts
Experiential	( )	E. expressed emotion
Multigenerational	( )	F. boundaries/hierarchies
Psychoeducational	( )	H. circular questioning
		I. power/control

Identify the Use of Children in Therapy

Bowen Systems	( )	A. Include to change family boundaries
Symbolic-Experiential	( )	B. Typically exclude from session to convey that they are not to blame
Structural	( )	C. Include to analyze projective transference of parents
Object Relations	( )	D. Include for spontaneity

Purpose of Interpretations

Symbolic-Experiential	( )	A. Elicit repressed or forgotten material
Object Relations	( )	B. Increase anxiety
Strategic	( )	C. Increase empathy
Satir	( )	D. Reframe problematic behavior

Role of Anxiety in Treatment

Symbolic-Experiential	( )	A. Avoid at all costs
Psychoeducational	( )	B. Regulate to moderate the level of motivation but not enough to interfere with intellectual functioning
Bowen Systems	( )	C. Increase to access unexpressed emotion

☐ Short Answer

1. Which therapies are associated with in-session versus out-of-session tasks? Explain the consistency of task assignment type with the underlying theoretical tenets.
2. Define Bowen's concept of differentiation, and describe how it relates to the objective of therapy.
3. Define homeostasis, and describe how it relates to the notion of client resistance in individual psychotherapy.
4. Define enactment. What therapy model is it associated with, and what is its purpose?
5. Define the battle for structure and battle for initiative.
6. Identify the four stages of treatment used in the Psychoeducational approach for the treatment of schizophrenia.
7. List at least three parenting traits associated with antisocial boys.

8. Define expressed emotion, and discuss its relationship to the Psychoeducational approach.
9. How does Behavior Parent Training utilize the marital relationship in its development of a treatment plan for the child?
10. Define enmeshment and disengagement. What type of boundary is associated with each?
11. What is the relationship between Strategic's "social stage" and Structural's "joining and accommodation?"
12. Define invariant prescription, and identify the associated model.
13. Both Strategic and MRI use strategic tasks to alter behaviors surrounding the presenting problem, yet they differ in its intended degree of influence per task; describe this difference and why it exists.
14. Define positive connotation and describe its use in Systemic Family Therapy.

Answers

1. A	16. C	31. A
2. D	17. D	32. C
3. C	18. D	33. A
4. B	19. C	34. B
5. C	20. C	35. C
6. D	21. B	36. C
7. A	22. C	37. C
8. A	23. A	38. B
9. A	24. D	39. A
10. B	25. B	40. A
11. A	26. C	
12. A	27. D	
13. B	28. D	
14. C	29. C	
15. A	30. D	

REFERENCES

Alexander, J., & Parsons, B. (1982). *Functional family therapy.* Monterey, CA: Brooks Cole.

Anderson, C. M. (1983). A psychoeducational program for families of patients with schizophrenia. In W. R. McFarlane (Ed.), *Family therapy in schizophrenia* (pp. 99–116). New York: Guilford.

[E]Anderson, C. M., Reiss, D. J., & Hogarty, G. E. (1986). *Schizophrenia and the family: A practitioner's guide to psychoeducation and management.* New York: Guilford.

Avis, J. M. (1985). The politics of functional family therapy: A feminist critique. *Journal of Marital and Family Therapy, 11,* 127–138.

Avis, J. M. (1996). Deconstructing gender in family therapy. In F. P. Piercy, D. H. Sprenkle, & J. L. Wetchler (Eds.), *Family therapy sourcebook* (2nd ed., pp. 220–255). New York: Guilford.

Bandler, R., & Grinder, J. (1979). *Frogs into princes.* Moab, UT: Real People Press.

Bandura, A. (1978). The self-system in reciprocal determinism. *American Psychologist, 33,* 344–358.

Bandura, A. (1982). Self-efficacy mechanisms in human agency. *American Psychologist, 37,* 122–147.

Barton, C., & Alexander, J. (1981). Functional Family Therapy. In A. S. Gurman & D. P. Kniskern (Eds.), *Handbook of family therapy* (Vol. I, pp. 403–443). New York: Brunner/Mazel.

Bateson, G. (1972). *Steps to an ecology of mind.* New York: Ballantine.

Bateson, G. (1979). *Mind and nature.* New York: E. P. Dutton.

Baucom, D. H., & Epstein, N. (1990). *Cognitive-behavioral marital therapy.* New York: Brunner/Mazel.

[E]Bodin, A. M. (1981). The interactional view: Family therapy approaches of the mental research institute. In A. S. Gurman & D. P. Kniskern (Eds.), *Handbook of family therapy* (Vol. I, pp. 267–309). New York: Brunner/Mazel.

[E]Boscolo, L., Cecchin, G., Hoffman, L., & Penn, P. (1987). *Milan systemic family therapy.* New York: Basic Books.

Boszormenyi-Nagy, I., & Ulrich, D. N. (1981). Contextual family therapy. In A. S. Gurman & D. P. Kniskern (Eds.), *Handbook of family therapy* (pp. 159–186). New York: Brunner/Mazel.

Brown, G. W., Birley, J. L. T., & Wing, J. K. (1972). Influence of family life on the course of schizophrenic illness: A replication. *British Journal of Psychiatry, 121,* 241–258.

F = Family therapy research and outcome

G = General texts and sourcebooks

E = Essential reading

B = Beneficial reading

Brown, G. W., Monck, E. M., Carstairs, G. M., & Wing, J. K. (1962). Influence of family life on the course of schizophrenic illness. *British Journal of Preventative and Social Medicine, 16,* 55–68.

Carter, B., & McGoldrick, M. (1988). *The changing family life cycle: A framework for family therapy* (2nd ed.). Boston: Allyn & Bacon.

Cashdon, S. (1988). *Object relations therapy: Using the relationship.* New York: Norton.

Crane, D. R. (1996). *Fundamentals of Marital Therapy.* New York: Brunner/Mazel.

Dattilio, F. M. (1998). *Case studies in couples and family therapy: Systemic and cognitive perspectives.* New York: Guilford.

Dattilio, F. M., & Padesky, C. A. (1990). *Cognitive therapy with couples.* Sarasota, FL: Professional Resource Exchange, Inc.

[E]de Shazer, S. (1985). *Keys to solution in brief therapy.* New York: Norton.

[E]de Shazer, S. (1988). *Clues: Investigating solutions in brief therapy.* New York: Norton.

[B]Duhl, B. S., & Duhl, F. J. (1981). Integrative family therapy. In A. S. Gurman & D. P. Kniskern (Eds.), *Handbook of family therapy* (pp. 483–513). New York: Brunner/Mazel.

Duhl, F. J., Kantor, D., & Duhl, B. S. (1973). Learning, space, and action in family therapy: A primer of sculpture. In D. Bloch (Ed.), *Techniques of family psychotherapy* (pp. 47–63). New York: Grune & Stratton.

Epstein, N. B., Baucom, D. H., & Daiuto, A. (1997). Cognitive-behavioral couples therapy. In W. K. Halford and H. J. Markman (Eds.), *Clinical handbook of marriage and couples interventions* (pp. 415–449). New York: Wiley & Sons.

[E]Falloon, I. R. H. (1991). Behavioral family therapy. In A. S. Gurman & D. P. Kniskern (Eds.), *Handbook of family therapy* (Vol. II, pp. 65–95). New York: Brunner/Mazel.

[B]Falloon, I. R. H., Boyd, J. L., & McGill, C. W. (Eds.). (1984). *Family care of schizophrenia.* New York: Guilford.

[E]Fisch, R., Weakland, J., & Segal, L. (1982). *The tactics of change.* San Francisco: Jossey Bass.

Fish, V. (1993). Poststructuralism in family therapy: Interrogating the narrative/conversational mode. *Journal of Marital and Family Therapy, 19*(3), 221–232.

Fontes, L. A., & Thomas, V. (1996). Cultural issues in family therapy. In F. P. Piercy, D. H. Sprenkle, & J. L. Wetcher (Eds.), *Family therapy sourcebook* (pp. 256–282). New York: Guilford.

[E]Framo, J. L. (1992). *Family of origin therapy: An intergenerational approach.* New York: Brunner/Mazel.

Goldstein, M. J., Rodnick, E. H., Evans, J. R., May, P. R., & Steinberg, M. (1978). Drug and family therapy in the aftercare treatment of acute schizophrenia. *Archives of General Psychiatry, 35,* 1169–1177.

[B]Greenberg, L. S., & Johnson, S. M. (1988). *Emotionally focused therapy for couples.* New York: Guilford.

[G]Griffin, W. A. (1993). *Family therapy: Fundamentals of theory and practice.* New York: Brunner/Mazel.

Grove, D., & Haley, J. (1993). *Conversations on therapy.* New York: Norton.

[E]Haley, J. (1963). *Strategies of psychotherapy.* New York: Grune and Stratton.

[B]Haley, J. (1967). *Advanced techniques of hypnosis and therapy: Selected papers of Milton H. Erickson, M.D.* New York: Grune & Stratton.

[B]Haley, J. (1973). *Uncommon therapy: The psychiatric techniques of Milton H. Erickson, M.D.* New York: Norton.

[E]Haley, J. (1980). *Leaving home.* New York: McGraw-Hill.

Haley, J. (1981). *Reflections of therapy and other essays.* Chevy Chase, MD: Jossey-Bass.

[E]Haley, J. (1984). *Ordeal therapy: Unusual ways to change behavior.* San Francisco: Jossey-Bass.

[E]Haley, J. (1987). *Problem-solving therapy for effective family therapy* (2nd ed.). San Francisco: Jossey-Bass.

[B]Hall, C. M. (1983). *The Bowen family theory and its uses.* New York: Aronson.

Hardy, K. V. (1989). The theoretical myth of sameness: A critical issue in family therapy treatment and training. In G. W. Saba, B. M. Karrer, & K. V. Hardy (Eds.), *Minorities and family therapy*. Binghamton, NY: Haworth.

Hare-Mustin, R. T. (1978). A feminist approach to family therapy. *Family Process, 17*, 181–194.

[B]Hoffman, L. (1981). *Foundation of family therapy*. New York: Basic Books.

Jackson, D. D. (1960). *The etiology of schizophrenia*. New York: Basic Books.

Jackson, D. D. (1964). *Myths of madness*. New York: Macmillan.

Kaplan, H. S. (1974). *The new sex therapy*. New York: Brunner/Mazel.

Kaplan, H. S. (1987). *The illustrated manual of sex therapy* (2nd ed.). New York: Brunner/Mazel.

[B]Kempler, W. (1981). *Experiential psychotherapy with families*. New York: Brunner/Mazel.

Lamb, S. (1991). Acts without agents: An analysis of linguistic avoidance in journal articles of men who batter women. *American Journal of Orthopsychiatry, 61*, 250–257.

Levant, R. (1984). *Family therapy: A comparative overview*. Englewood Cliffs, NJ: Prentice-Hall.

Linn, M. W., Caffey, E. M., Klett, C. J., Hogarty, G. E., & Lamb, R. (1979). Day treatment and psychotropic drugs in the aftercare of schizophrenic patients. *Archives of General Psychiatry, 36*, 1055–1066.

Linn, M. W., Klett, C. J., & Caffey, E. M. (1980). Foster home characteristics and psychiatric patient outcome. *Archives of General Psychiatry, 37*, 129–132.

LoPiccolo, J., & LoPiccolo, L. (1978). *Handbook of sex therapy*. New York: Plenum.

[B]Madanes, C. (1981). *Strategic family therapy*. San Francisco: Jossey-Bass.

[E]Madanes, C. (1984). *Behind the one-way mirror: Advances in the practice of strategic therapy*. San Francisco: Jossey-Bass.

[B]Madanes, C. (1990). *Sex, love, and violence: Strategies for transformation*. New York: Norton.

Madanes, C. (1991). Strategic family therapy. In A. S. Gurman & D. P. Kniskern (Eds.), *Handbook of family therapy* (Vol. II, pp. 396–416). New York: Brunner/Mazel.

Masters, W. H., & Johnson, V. E. (1970). *Human sexual inadequacy*. Boston: Little, Brown.

[E]McDaniel, S., Hepworth, J., & Doherty, W. (1992). *Medical family therapy*. New York: Basic Books.

McGoldrick, M., Anderson, C. M., & Walsh, F. (1989). Women in families and family therapy. In M. McGoldrick, C. M. Anderson, & F. Walsh (Eds.), *Women in families: A framework for family therapy* (pp. 3–15). New York: Norton.

[E]Minuchin, S. (1974). *Families and family therapy*. Cambridge, MA: Harvard University Press.

[B]Minuchin, S., Rosman, B. L., & Baker, L. (1978). *Psychosomatic families: Anorexia nervosa in context*. Cambridge, MA: Harvard University Press.

Nichols, W. C. (1996). *Treating people in families: An integrative framework*. New York: Guilford.

[E]Ogden, T. H. (1982). *Projective identification and psychotherapeutic technique*. New York: Aronson.

Parsons, T., & Bales, R. F. (1955). *Family socialization and interaction*. Glencoe, IL: Free Press.

[E]Patterson, G. R. (1971). *Families: Applications of social learning to family life*. Champaign, IL: Research Press.

Patterson, G. R., & Chamberlain, P. (1988). Treatment process: A problem at three levels. In L. C. Wynne (Ed.), *The state of the art in family therapy research* (pp. 189–223). New York: Norton.

[E]Patterson, G. R., Reid, J. B., & Dishion, T. J. (1992). *Antisocial boys*. Eugene, OR: Castalia.

Pinsof, W. M. (1995). *Integrative problem-centered therapy: A synthesis of family, individual, and biological therapies*. New York: Basic Books.

[B]Rolland, J. S. (1994). *Helping families with chronic and life-threatening disorders*. New York: Basic Books.

Satir, V. M. (1975a). Intervention for congruence. In V. Satir, J. Stachowiak, & H. A. Tashman. *Helping families to change* (pp. 79–104). New York: Aronson.

Satir, V. M. (1975b). You as a change agent. In V. Satir, J. Stachowiak, & H. A. Tashman. *Helping families to change* (pp. 37–62). New York: Aronson.

[E]Satir, V. M., & Baldwin, M. (1983). *Satir step by step: A guide to creating change in families.* Palo Alto, CA: Science and Behavior Books.

Satir, V., Stachowiak, J., & Tashman, H. A. (1975). *Helping families to change.* New York: Aronson.

Scharff, D., & Scharff, J. (1987). *Object relations family therapy.* New York: Aronson.

[B]Scharff, D, & Scharff, J. (1991). *Object relations couple therapy.* Northvale, NJ: Aronson.

[B]Schnarch, D. M. (1991). *Constructing the sexual crucible: An integration of sexual and marital therapy.* New York: Norton.

Schwartz, R. (1994). *Internal family systems therapy.* New York: Guilford Press.

Schwartzmann, J. (1983). Family ethnography: A tool for clinicians. In C. J. Falicov (Ed.), *Cultural perspectives in family therapy.* Rockville, MD: Aspen.

[E]Segal, L. (1991). Brief therapy: The MRI approach. In A. S. Gurman & D. P. Kniskern (Eds.), *Handbook of family therapy* (Vol. II, pp. 171–199). New York: Brunner/Mazel.

[B]Siegel, J. (1992). *Repairing intimacy: An object relations approach to couples therapy.* Northvale, NJ: Aronson.

[E]Stanton, M. D. (1981). Strategic approaches to family therapy. In A. S. Gurman & D. P. Kniskern (Eds.), *Handbook of family therapy* (Vol. I, pp. 361–402). New York: Brunner/Mazel.

Thibaut, J., & Kelly, H. H. (1959). *The social psychology of groups.* New York: Wiley.

[E]Tomm, K. (1984a). One perspective on the Milan systemic approach: Part I. Overview of development, theory, and practice. *Journal of Marital and Family Therapy, 10,* 113–125.

[E]Tomm, K. (1984b). One perspective on the Milan systemic approach: Part II. Description of session format, interviewing style, and interventions. *Journal of Marital and Family Therapy, 10,* 253–271.

[B]Tomm, K. (1988). Interventive interviewing, Part III: Intending to ask linear, circular, strategic, or reflexive questions. *Family Process, 27,* 1–15.

Vaughn, C., & Leff, J. P. (1976). The measurement of expressed emotion in the families of psychiatric patients. *British Journal of Clinical and Social Psychology, 15,* 157–165.

Vaughn, C. E., Snyder, K. S., Jones, S., Freeman, W. B., & Falloon, I. R. H. (1984). Family factors in schizophrenic relapse: A California replication of the British research on expressed emotion. *Archives of General Psychiatry, 41,* 1169–1177.

von Bertalanffy, L. (1968). *General system theory.* New York: George Braziller.

Wahler, R., & Dumas, J. (1989). Attentional problems in dysfunctional mother-child interactions. *Psychological Bulletin, 105,* 116–130.

[B]Watzlawick, P. (1976). *How real is real?* New York: Random House.

[E]Watzlawick, P. (1978). *The language of change: Elements of therapeutic communication.* New York: Basic Books.

[B]Watzlawick, P. (Ed.). (1984). *The invented reality: How do we know what we believe we know? Contributions to constructivism.* New York: Norton.

[E]Watzlawick, P. (1990). *Munchhausen's pigtail.* New York: Norton.

[B]Watzlawick, P. A., Beavin, J. H., & Jackson, D. D. (1967). *Pragmatics of human communication.* New York: Norton.

[E]Watzlawick, P., Weakland, J. H., & Fisch, R. (1974). *Change: Principles of problem formation and problem resolution.* New York: Norton.

Weiner, N. (1961). *Cybernetics, or control and communication in the animal and the machine.* Cambridge, MA: MIT Press.

Whitaker, C. A. (1975). Psychotherapy of the absurd: With a special emphasis on the psychotherapy of aggression. *Family Process, 14,* 1–16.

Whitaker, C. A. (1976). A family is a four-dimensional relationship. In P. J. Guerin (Ed.), *Family therapy: Theory and practice* (pp. 154–164). New York: Gardner.

[E]Whitaker, C. A., & Keith, D. V. (1981). Symbolic-experiential family therapy. In A. S. Gurman & D. P. Kniskern (Eds.), *Handbook of family therapy* (pp. 187–225). New York: Brunner/Mazel.

[E]White, M., & Epston, D. (1990). *Narrative means to therapeutic ends.* New York: Norton.

[F]Wynne, L. (1988). *The state of the art in family therapy research.* New York: Norton.

ADDITIONAL SUGGESTED READING

[F]Alexander, J. F., Holtzworth-Munroe, A., & Jameson, P. (1994). The process and outcome of marriage and family therapy: Research review and evaluation. In A. E. Bergin & S. L. Garfield (Eds.), *Handbook of Psychotherapy and Behavior Change* (4th ed., pp. 595–630). New York: Wiley.

American Association for Marriage and Family Therapy. (1991). *AAMFT Code of Ethics*. Washington, DC: AAMFT.

[B]Anonymous. (1972). Differentiation of self in one's family. In J. Framo (Ed.), *Family interaction* (pp. 529–547). New York: Springer.

[B]Aponte, H. J., & VanDeusen, J. M. (1981). Structural family therapy. In A. S. Gurman & D. P. Kniskern (Eds.), *Handbook of family therapy* (Vol. 1, pp. 310–360). New York: Brunner/Mazel.

[G]Becvar, D. S., & Becvar, R. J. (1993). *Family therapy: A systemic integration* (2nd ed.). Boston: Allyn & Bacon.

[B]Boszormenyi-Nagy, I., & Krasner, B. R. (1986). *Between give and take: A clinical guide to contextual therapy*. New York: Brunner/Mazel.

[E]Bowen, M. (1976). Theory in the practice of psychotherapy. In P. J. Guerin (Ed.), *Family therapy: Theory and practice* (pp. 42–90). New York: Gardner.

[B]Carter, E., & Orfanidis, M. M. (1976). Family therapy with one person and the family therapist's own family. In P. J. Guerin (Ed.), *Family therapy: Theory and practice* (pp. 193–219). New York: Gardner.

[B]Colapinto, J. (1991). Structural family therapy. In A. S. Gurman & D. P. Kniskern (Eds.), *Handbook of family therapy* (Vol. II, pp. 417–443). New York: Brunner/Mazel.

Davidson, M. (1983). *Uncommon sense*. Los Angeles: J. P. Tarcher.

[E]de Shazer, S. (1984). The death of resistance. *Family Process, 23*, 79–93.

[B]de Shazer, S. (1991). *Putting difference to work*. New York: Norton.

[E]Eisenstein, H. (1983). *Contemporary feminist thought*. Boston: Hall.

[E]Falicov, C. J. (1988). Learning to think culturally. In H. A. Liddle, D. C. Breunlin, & R. C. Schwartz (Eds.), *Handbook of family therapy training and supervision*. New York: Guilford.

F = Family therapy research and outcome
G = General texts and sourcebooks
E = Essential reading
B = Beneficial reading

[B]Falloon, I. R. H. (Ed.). (1988). *Handbook of behavioral family therapy.* New York: Guilford.
Falloon, I. R. H., Boyd, J. L., McGill, C. W., Williamson, M., Razaniz, J., Moss, H. B., Gilderman, A. M., & Simpson, G. M. (1985). Family management in the prevention of morbidity of schizophrenia: Clinical outcome of a two-year longitudinal study. *Archives of General Psychiatry, 42,* 887–896.
[E]Framo, J. L. (1982). *Explorations in marital and family therapy: Selected papers of James L. Framo.* New York: Springer.
[G]Goldenberg, I., & Goldenberg, H. (1996). *Family therapy: An overview* (4th ed.). Pacific Grove, CA: Brooks Cole.
[E]Goldstein, M. J., & Stachan, A. M. (1987). The family and schizophrenia. In T. Jacob (Ed.), *Family interaction and psychopathology: Theories, methods, and findings* (pp. 481–508). New York: Plenum.
Goodrich, T. J. (1991). *Women and power: Perspectives for family therapy.* New York: Norton.
[B]Gordon, S. B., & Davidson, N. (1981). Behavioral parent training. In A. S. Gurman & D. P. Kniskern (Eds.), *Handbook of family therapy* (Vol. I, pp. 517–555). New York: Brunner/Mazel.
Gray, W., Duhl, F. J., & Rizzo, N. D. (1969). *General systems theory and psychiatry.* Boston: Little, Brown.
[B]Guerin, P. J., Fay, L., Burden, S., & Kautto, J. (1987). *The evaluation and treatment of marital conflict: A four stage approach.* New York: Basic Books.
[E]Haley, J. (1986). *The power tactics of Jesus Christ* (2nd ed.). Rockville, MD: The Triangle Press.
[B]Haley, J. (1988). Reflections on therapy supervision. In H. Liddle, D. Breunlin, & R. Schwartz (Eds.), *Handbook of family therapy training and supervision.* New York: Guilford.
[F]Hazelrigg, M. D., Cooper, H. M., & Bourdin, C. M. (1987). Evaluating the effectiveness of family therapies: An integrative review and analysis. *Psychological Bulletin, 101,* 428–442.
Heiman, J. R., LoPiccolo, L., & LoPiccolo, J. (1981). The treatment of sexual dysfunction. In A. S. Gurman & D. P. Kniskern (Eds.), *Handbook of family therapy* (Vol. I, pp. 592–630). New York: Brunner/Mazel.
[B]Hooley, J. M. (1985). Expressed emotion: A review of the critical literature. *Clinical Psychology Review, 5,* 119–139.
Jacobson, N. S., & Christensen, A. (1996). *Integrative couple therapy.* New York: Norton.
[E]Kerr, M., & Bowen, M. (1988). *Family evaluation.* New York: Norton.
[E]Leff, J. P., & Vaughn, C. (1985). *Expressed emotion in families: Its significance for mental illness.* New York: Guilford.
[B]McGoldrick, M., & Gerson, R. (1985). *Genograms in family assessment.* New York: Norton.
[E]McGoldrick, M., Giordano, J., & Pearce, J. K. (1996). *Ethnicity and family therapy* (2nd ed.). New York: Guilford.
[B]McGoldrick, M., Anderson, C., & Walsh, F. (Eds.). (1988). *Women in families: A framework for family therapy.* New York: Norton.
[B]Minuchin, S. (1979). Constructing a therapeutic reality. In E. Kaufman and P. Kaufmann (Eds.), *Family therapy of drug and alcohol abuse* (pp. 3–18). New York: Gardner Press.
[E]Minuchin, S., & Fishman, H. C. (1981). *Family therapy techniques.* Cambridge, MA: Harvard University Press.
[B]Minuchin, S., Montalvo, B., Guerney, B. G., Rosman, B. L., & Schumer, F. (1967). *Families of the slums: An exploration of their structure and treatment.* New York: Basic Books.
[E]Mirkin, M. P. (Ed.). (1994). *Woman in context: Toward a feminist reconstruction of psychotherapy.* New York: Guilford.
[B]Napier, A. Y., & Whitaker, C. A. (1978). *The family crucible.* New York: Harper & Row.
[G]Nichols, M. P., & Schwartz, R. C. (1995). *Family therapy: Concepts and methods* (3rd ed.). Boston: Allyn & Bacon.
[B]O'Hanlon, W. H. (1987). *Taproots: Underlying principles of Milton Erickson's therapy and hypnosis.* New York: Norton.

[E]O'Hanlon, W. H., & Weiner-Davis, M. (1989). *In search of solutions: A new direction in psychotherapy.* New York: Norton.
[E]Papero, D. V. (1990). *Bowen family systems theory.* Needham Heights, MA: Allyn & Bacon.
[E]Patterson, G. R. (1982). *Coercive family process.* Eugene, OR: Castalia.
[G]Piercy, F. P., Sprenkle, D. H., & Wetcher, J. L. (1996). *Family therapy sourcebook.* New York: Guilford.
[F]Pinsof, W., & Wynne, L. (1995). The efficacy of marital and family therapy: An empirical overview, conclusions, and recommendations. In W. Pinsof & L. Wynne (Eds.), Family therapy effectiveness: Current research and theory (pp. 585–613) [Special issue]. *Journal of Marital and Family Therapy, 21*(4). Washington: JMFT Press.
[F]Pinsof, W., & Wynne, L. (Eds.). (1995). Family therapy effectiveness [Special issue]. *Journal of Marital and Family Therapy, 21*(4). Washington: JMFT Press.
[B]Rabkin, R. (1977). *Strategic psychotherapy.* New York: Basic Books.
Rossi, E. (1980). *Collected papers of Milton Erickson on hypnosis* (4 volumes). New York: Irvington.
[B]Saba, G. W., Karrer, B. M., & Hardy, K. V. (1989). *Minorities and family therapy.* Binghamton, NY: Haworth.
[E]Satir, V. M. (1988). *The new peoplemaking.* Palo Alto, CA: Science and Behavior Books.
[E]Scharff, J. S. (Ed.). (1991). *Foundations of object relations family therapy.* Northvale, NJ: Aronson.
[E]Selvini-Palazzoli, M., Boscolo, L., Cecchin, G., & Prata, G. (1978). *Paradox and counterparadox.* New York: Aronson.
[E]Selvini-Palazzoli, M., Cirillo, S., Selvini, M., & Sorrentino, A. M. (1989). *Family games: General models of psychotic processes in the family.* New York: Norton.
[F]Shadish, W. R., Montgomery, L. M., Wilson, P., Wilson, M. R., Bright, I., & Okwumabua, T. (1993). The effects of family and marital psychotherapies: A meta-analysis. *Journal of Consulting and Clinical Psychology, 59,* 883–893.
[B]Slipp, S. (1988). *Technique and practice of object relations family therapy.* New York: Aronson.
[B]Tomm, K. (1985). Circular questioning: A multifaceted clinical tool. In D. Campbell & R. Draper (Eds.), *Application of systemic family therapy: The Milan method* (pp. 33–45). New York: Grune & Stratton.
[E]Webster-Stratton, C., & Herber, M. (1994). *Troubled families: Problem children.* New York: Wiley.
[B]White, M. (1986). Negative explanation, restraint, and double description: A template for family therapy. *Family Process, 25*(2), 169–184.

INDEX